CAGED
NO MORE

LEARNING TO BE
SET FREE

A Journey into a Life of Many *Scars* That God

Turned into *Stars*

Rose Hogans

ISBN 978-1-68526-401-7 (Paperback)
ISBN 979-8-88644-474-2 (Hardcover)
ISBN 978-1-68526-402-4 (Digital)

Covenant Books
11661 Hwy 707
Murrells Inlet, SC 29576
www.covenantbooks.com

I dedicate this book

- to my Lord and savior, Jesus Christ, who saw me and my many flaws and undone conditions, He picked me up, and allowed me to live. He has always been there for me, telling me: "The greatest gift you can give is your story!"
- to my late husband, Billy Hogans, who has always inspired me to tell my story saying many need to hear it.
- to my wonderful children Malinda and Brian. Thank you for allowing me the opportunity to be a part of your lives.
- to my wonderful son, Mickis, who has always been with me through thick and thin, encouraging me to write, speak, and grow.
- to my grandson Mickis Jr., who has always listened to me with my many ideas and creativity, always there to give me a helping hand with things around the house, spelling and pronouncing words, and never being too busy to talk with me. He has been my rock so many times.
- to my grandson Jaden for taking the time to always draw and sketch out pictures for me.

- to my sister Lynda, who has taken the time to help me and listen to my stories of abuse, even when it hurt her to hear them.
- to my sister Gwen, who has been right there crying with me and listening to me; cheering me on through the process of writing this book; gladly telling people, "My sister is writing a book"; calling things to be before they happen; and being one of my biggest cheerleaders.
- to my sister Mary, who would allow me to talk with her anytime.
- to my sweet butterfly (Jamie) who has always inspired me through her many actions. When she would always say I was helping her, she was helping me.
- to my sweet sunshine (Kim) who was always there to share her open arms and her heart with me.
- to the many others who believed in me, encouraged me, and pulled me on to move forward. Thank you!

I dedicate this book to you if you have been abused physically, mentally, emotionally, or sexually. God can help you through!

> *Nothing is too hard for him.* (Jeremiah 32:27 NIV; paraphrased)

Cast all anxiety [worries, cares, and fears] on him because he cares for you. (1 Peter 5:7 NIV)

He is healing me from inside out, he is no respecter of persons. (Acts 10:34 KJV; paraphrased)

Prayerfully, you begin your healing process as you read my true story! Love you all. Please continue to pray for me! MAY GOD BLESS EACH OF YOU.

FOREWORD

Allow me to say a few words about Rose.

She touches people daily in an extraordinary way. Whether we are out shopping or just having lunch at one of our favorite venues, she will spot someone who's not having a good day and give them a hug and encouraging words and pray for them. She always leaves a place or person better than before we entered the arena. Her compassion and love for people are heart felt and genuine.

There's been many examples where because of one person, God spared the people. Because of one, a legacy was started. Because of one being obedient to the voice of God, several family members got saved, repented, and baptized in the name of Jesus Christ for the remission of sins and received the Holy Ghost with the evidence of speaking in tongues (Acts 2:38–40 KJV). Well, thank you, Rose Hogans, for being "that one"! This book is powerful and heartfelt.

—Lynda Brown

M y name is Rose J. Hogans. I was born and raised in Chicago, Illinois, at Cook County Hospital on March 29, 1960, to Charlie and Merlean Brown. As I open myself up and tell my story, I hope and pray that you, too, will receive healing. "Then you will know the truth, and the truth will set you free" (John 8:32 NIV).

My earliest memory of being a little girl at the age of four was being touched by an old man whom my parents hired to babysit me and my sister Lynda while they went out to the bar. She was only two years old during this time. He would put me on one side of him, Lynda on the other side. He would take his hands and rub our legs up and down and tell us things that no young girls should ever be told. When my parents came back from the bar, we told them what happened to us. My dad, angry and distraught, beat up that old man so badly that he crawled out of our house that night.

A few months later, I remember seeing my father cry because his father passed away. At that time, I didn't understand why he was crying, because I was so young. Shortly after this, my dad would take me and my sister Lynda to the bar once or twice a week, telling me and her to hit it, which was our cue to dance, and we would be in front of all these men at the bar. Being young girls, we just did what we were told to do, and my dad always thought it was funny because his little girls could dance so well. I remember many times we would fall asleep there at the bar in one of the booths because my parents would be drinking and my dad gambling.

My parents loved the oldies such as B. B. King, Bobby "Blue" Bland, Gladys Knight, and many more. My parents drank a lot of hard liquor such as gin, Crown Royal, vodka, E & J. They also drank a lot of beer and smoked cigarettes. My mother's choice of cigarettes was Winston, and my father's choice of smoke was Benson & Hedges. They both smoked and drank all my life, as far as I could remember. They did this so frequently. They got to the point they were smoking two or three packs of cigarettes a day and drinking hard liquor daily. My sister and I grew up listening to them cussing at each other and fighting almost daily. I remember us moving around a lot because my dad would get paid on Fridays and go to the bar and he would gamble away his paycheck, sometimes not even bothering to come home until Sunday. When he came home, he would be broke and proceed to take his anger out on my mother, hitting her and cussing her out because he had lost all his money like it was her fault. I remember so many times us not having food to eat. My mother would take us to the store so she could get herself a pack of cigarettes and get myself and my sister Lynda a Suzy Q, which we both had to share because my mother had just enough money for only that. We never stayed in one place too long—two to three months at the most because we constantly got evicted for not paying the rent.

We never had stable friends. We lived in Chicago until I was about age ten, my dad with the same pattern: getting paid on Fridays, gambling away his paycheck, and coming home, beating my mom. I got hit on many occasions, trying to get between them to stop my mother from being hit. There was never money for rent, food, or electricity. I don't ever remember getting new clothes and shoes or having toys, never having a doll or girly things. We always wore hand-me-downs. Sometime later, my mom went to work at GMC, working on the assembly line, putting car parts on GMC vehicles, just to have some type of escape and to help make ends meet. However, my dad would continually hound her for her money because he gambled and drank his away. So I had to take care of myself and my sister Lynda.

Sometime later, my mother got pregnant with my baby sister, Gwen, so she worked until she had to stop a few months before having my little sister. Three months after the birth of my little sister, she went back to work. It was short-lived because I had to watch my sisters at night and still be ready for school the next morning.

It was difficult on us all—my mom trying to work with both of us being in school and my dad drinking and gambling nightly. She had no babysitter to watch my little sister Gwen. My mom was still dealing with beatings from my dad! She had to come off her job. Things got so tight that she sent me and my sister Lynda to Johnsville, Arkansas (I was around ten and my sister was eight) to live with our grandparents (her mother and her father) because she had three mouths to feed and the beatings continued to get worse.

After about a year and a half of me and my sister Lynda being in Johnsville, Arkansas, with my grandparents, my parents wound up moving to Crossett, Arkansas, where my dad's family lived, and it was about a little over an hour from the house of my mother's parent.

We would live here and there for a while around eleven and a half. I remember my parents getting a three-bedroom mobile-trailer home. I was happy because it appeared we had a stable home we thought!

My parents were still drinking, smoking, and fighting all the time. I remember telling my mother about an older man who was my father's friend trying to talk to me. My dad did not believe my mother, so he beat her and said I was lying. So when things would happen, I never told my parents, for fear of my mother getting beaten and my dad not believing me!

I remember my sister Lynda and I started going to church to get out of the house because my dad was so strict and did not allow us to go anywhere but school and right around our home. So we would go to church every Sunday, Lynda and I. My parents never took us. We decided to go on our own, and we loved it.

I remember, at the age of thirteen, going to this holiness church, which we attended faithfully. I went forth to get prayer for my family, and someone laid hands on me, and I fell back on the floor and started to speak in tongues. I spoke in tongues for a long time. My sister Lynda ran to the altar, asking them, "What are you guys doing to my sister?" They explained to her that I had received the Holy Ghost, with the evidence of speaking in tongues. "*All of them were filled with the Holy Ghost and began to speak in other tongues as the Spirit enabled them*" (Acts 2:4 NIV). I did not understand what happened to me, but it felt really good. So now, at the age of thirteen, I had God's spirit inside me without the understanding and knowledge of what I had.

FIRST BOYFRIEND

Now, at the age of fourteen, I had my first boyfriend his name was Ricky. We were only able to see each other at school and at church because my dad was so strict. Ricky was two years older than me. I also started to play tennis, which I really enjoyed. I played for about two years, and my parents never went to any of my tennis matches. I could never go to any away matches because my dad was so strict.

I wished my parents would have come to see me play. But they never did; they always made excuses. I really desired to make this a career.

While dating this young man, we started skipping classes so we could spend time together. Each day was different; I would ride the bus to school, maybe go to one period then skip the second period. Ricky and I would hang out at his aunt's house; she lived across the street from the school—still no sex at all, some kissing and hugging. We were glad to be together. I never skipped more than one class a day, and I never missed tennis practice or matches! So the principal started seeing my pattern and would see me walking to this house, throughout the day, across the street, when I should be in class. She called my parents because my pattern was skipping one class a day. I got busted! I remember seeing my dad's truck pull up at the school because my boyfriend's aunt lived across the street facing the school. My dad took Lynda out of class, asking her where I was. She never told them anything (thank you, sissy, for always having my back). So I just went out of the apartment and walked across to the school, scared to death!

Let's just say I was put on restriction for thirty days, then whipped. I could only go to school and maybe tennis, depending on how my father felt. I could not go outside after school. So I had to stand in the window and watch all my friends outside, enjoying themselves. We were still living in the mobile home, and my bedroom was in the back, so at night, my boyfriend would come and talk with me at my window for a little while because we both had school in the morning. So one night, I decided to allow my boyfriend to come inside the house after we talked at the back window for a few minutes and to lie on the bed with me—still no sex. This went on for a few weeks. He would lie with me, and we would cuddle and talk for a few hours. Then I would let him back out the side door, not thinking too much about it because my parents were always drinking, and they would normally pass out (which was an everyday routine).

So one night, after a few weeks of him coming in through the side door—I am around fifteen at this time— Mom heard a noise, which was me letting my boyfriend in through the side door. First, she yelled back to me and my sister Lynda, "What are you guys doing?" Then I heard her coming down the hallway. I put my boyfriend in my closet then jumped into the bed like I was asleep. She started snooping around because she discovered the side door was not closed tightly or locked. I told her I was letting out the cat (which we did not have). I forgot to lock the door; I was so scared. Then she opened the closet door, and my boyfriend was standing there with his hands behind his back, shaking like a leaf. She grabbed him by his collar and was dragging him up the hallway, trying to get my dad to wake up. It took her about seven calls before my dad woke up. As soon as she released Ricky, he shot out the side door, leaving his shoes at the door outside because he always pulled them off so you could not hear them squeaking on the floor as he was going in.

My dad jumped up. She was yelling at my dad, "Rose has a boy in this house!" He grabbed his shotgun and cocked it, went outside, looking for my boyfriend. I learned later on that Ricky told me he ran all the way home and did not stop. He lived about fifteen minutes away from me. My dad came back yelling and cursing, "Get up and get dressed, both of you I'm taking y'all to a bad-girl school." I was so scared. Now my sister Lynda did not do anything, but she got in trouble because she did not tell on me. My dad got a brown extension cord and beat the stew out of me. I had knots on my back, on my arms, and on my legs. He whipped me until he got tired, cussing me out and calling me names. Then he turned around and whipped my sister Lynda because of me. Sorry, sissy! I thought I was going to die. Now back on punishment again for another thirty days—only to school and back in the house for me with no more tennis for a while!

I was about fifteen and a half years old, still no sex, but still in trouble for something. So one day, my mom needed some cigarettes, and I volunteered to go walk to the store to get them for her, but I had to take my baby sister, Gwen, who was about two years old, with me.

So I started paying attention to the pattern. About every two days, my mom needed me to walk to the store, which was about a fifteen- to twenty-minute walk. That walk would be slower with my little sister accompanying me. So I told my boyfriend around about what time we would be walking so he could pick me up. We went to the store, got the items my mom needed, then we would go to this street called Lover's Lane (mind you, I had my little sister with me)! So we started making out, we put her in the front seat and gave her the keys to play with, and we had sex for the first time. We both were virgins! This was March 23. My sixteenth birthday was coming up on March 29.

The hardest thing for me was keeping my little sister Gwen's mouth shut because she kept saying, "If you don't take me with you, I'm going to tell mom your boyfriend had his booty in your booty." So I took her with me for a while to keep her quiet. I was off punishment, so as the months went on, I started playing tennis again, and I did not realize I did not have a cycle because I was so wrapped up in tennis that I didn't notice three months had gone by without my period or cycle. I had a feeling I was pregnant, but I hid it well. I was so afraid to tell my parents because I thought my dad would beat the baby out of my stomach or make me have an abortion.

My aunt Ruby came to visit us from Chicago about three months later. She kept staring at me but would not say anything. She finally told my mother, before she left to go back home to Chicago, "Rose is pregnant!" My mother said, "No, she isn't!" My auntie said, "Trust me, she is!"

My little sister, Gwen, had already told my mom about me and my boyfriend, but she did not believe her. So after Aunt Ruby left, a week later, my mom asked me when the last time I had my period or cycle. I told her it was about four to five months ago. She took me to the doctor, and of course, I was pregnant—five and a half months pregnant. I was still playing tennis and going to school. I hid it very well, but after they found out, my stomach just blew up. I was so afraid that my dad was going to make me have an abortion. So I kept going to school and stopped playing tennis and started working at Sonic part-time at night, after school, until I was about eight months and too big to get around. At about seven and a half months of my pregnancy, my parents made excuses for me to stay at home from school as punishment, and they were ashamed of me being pregnant. I never went to eleventh or twelfth grade. I had to babysit my little sister Gwen because my parents worked. I worked until I was around eight and a half months pregnant.

Now about my boyfriend Ricky (my son's dad), my father, Charlie, had threatened him, telling him if he came around me, that he was going to kill him. This happened on a few occasions, which I found out later. The only way I was able to see Ricky was when I was working at Sonic and going to school. He knew I was pregnant, but my father kept him away. I did not understand for a while why he did not come around, knowing we had a child on the way. I wanted him around for us to experience this together.

Two days before I went into the hospital, I became sick and started lying around. When I would use the restroom and wipe, it would be slimy, and I would see blood. But I didn't know what that meant. So I told my mother, and she told my dad, "We need to take Rose to the hospital."

So off we went, December 20, 1976, around 5:30 p.m. I was sixteen years old. We had to drive to Bastrop, Louisiana, which was about two hours away from our home, because our hospitals were not delivering babies in Crossett, Arkansas, at that time. So when we got to Bastrop, the doctors checked me out and admitted me to the hospital, saying, "She will be delivering very soon." My water never broke, and I didn't have much pain—just a little under my stomach.

The delivery was scary because I was sixteen and no one told me anything about having a baby. There was another lady in the room with me in the hospital, screaming and yelling that was her third child. She scared me more than anything. I remember going into the delivery room, getting ready to have my baby. The nurse and doctor were so kind, and they explained everything that would happen. So I remember the doctor telling me, "We will have to break your water, and we will tell you when to push." Everything happened so fast. I remember pushing about three to four times, and the baby came out crying with strong lungs. The doctor announced, "It's a boy." He weighed seven pounds and two ounces and was born on December 20, 1976, at

10:44 p.m. I never knew whether it would be a boy or a girl. I instantly fell in love with my son!

I was thankful for a healthy baby. My uncle Henry named my son Mickis Spalanie (after some famous writer). I was now a young mother with responsibilities to my child. I took a few months off to heal then went back to work at Sonic at night to be able to purchase formula and diapers for my son, and I babysat my little sister, Gwen, in the daytime. She was about three years old. I wanted to go back to school, but my parents wouldn't let me. My dad always reminded me how much of a failure I was, getting pregnant so young.

So I always kept my son quiet when my dad was around. My sister Lynda would watch Mickis while I worked at night. Mickis was such a good baby, always happy, and brought me much joy.

Merlean and Charlie Brown

ROSE HOGANS

What would you have done?

LOSING OUR HOME

When I was seventeen and a half, still not in school—working and taking care of my son—I could hear my father cussing and fighting my mother because of money. A few days later, my mother told us to pack our things, and we have to move. My parents were so far behind on the house payment that we were getting foreclosed on and that we had to move in a hurry. My dad packed up everything, and we moved to Johnsville, Arkansas, close to my mother's family.

We moved into a little two-bedroom house on my grandmother and grandfather's property, without a restroom or running water. This was a shocker to me and my sister Lynda because we were used to having a bathroom with running water and having our separate rooms. We slept in a bed together, me, her, and Mickis between us. My grandparents had a well on their property, so we had to pump the water and carry buckets to the house. We had to bathe in a round tin tub and heat the water to make it hot. We also had to use the same water to take baths in because the well was a little distance to walk back and forth. To use the restroom, we had to go outside to the outhouse, which was made of wood. At night, we had a bucket just to pee in, and we had to carry it out every morning to dump it. We had limited electricity, so we used a wood iron stove for heat, and my mom used it to cook. We learned how to cut wood daily for the stove. Coming from a place called home in Crossett, Arkansas, to a very small town in Johnsville, Arkansas, what a difference for us. But remember we stayed with my grandparents for about one and a half years, Lynda and me. The house was big and roomy, so we learned about cutting wood and pumping water from the well and using the outhouse for the restroom.

My dad was still very strict and still abusing my mom. They both were still heavy drinkers and smokers, and we still could not go anywhere. I remember asking my dad if Lynda and I could go to the little café across the way where the teenagers hung out to shoot pool and listen to music on the jukebox. I was eighteen, and my sister was sixteen, and I had a two-year-old son.

He kept making excuses. My sister Lynda and I were sitting on each side of my mom by the woodstove to keep warm, on the arms of a big recliner chair my mom was sitting in. Lynda was on her right side, and I was on her left side. My mom said, "Let them go. I will watch Mickis." My dad had a piece of iron in his hand that was used to stir the wood in a woodstove. He was bending down like he was going to open the door to the woodstove and turn the wood. He reached between Lynda and me and hit my mother in her forehead with that piece of iron and busted her head wide-open. Blood went everywhere like a fountain turned on, but it was red! You could see the bone in her forehead because the gash was so deep. She got hit because she asked him to let us go to the café! Then he would not let her or us out of the house to take her to the hospital. I remember pushing her out the back door so she wouldn't bleed to death. My sister Lynda ran to my grandparents' house and got my mom some help. The doctors put about seventeen to eighteen stitches on her forehead, inside out. The police wanted her to press charges against him, but she wouldn't. My mother's face was swollen for a few weeks. She went home after two days in the hospital. Things should have changed, but they didn't.

Some months later, my dad lost his job, so he started bootlegging, selling beer, hard liquor, and wine in a dry county. My mom worked on tomato farms, packing and grating tomatoes. I would go with her to make money sometimes if I had a babysitter.

Then it got to the point when my dad would not allow us to go anywhere unless we went with someone he knew. We had lots of traffic because of my dad's bootlegging. People (men) would always be around our house, drinking and smoking. There was one guy my dad knew, who hung around a lot, so my dad would allow us to go with him to the store and little café, and this guy started coming on to me when I was around eighteen and a half years old.

After my nineteenth birthday, I got a job in Warren (which was about twenty to thirty minutes away from Johnsville) at a company called Masonite, making wood floors. I had to catch rides to work with others for a few months until I made enough to purchase a little car. It was a Nova Vega for $500. I was so proud of the first car that I paid cash for. (Thank you, Jesus.)

Then I got into a two-bedroom house that I rented for $75 a month. At that time, there were these big butane tanks that would hold about one hundred pounds of propane, which cost about $50 a month, used for gas stoves. Electricity was about $40 a month, and we had an inside toilet with running water. I could take care of myself and my son. My sister Lynda and my mom would help me out with babysitting when I went to work Monday to Friday.

Mickis's dad, Ricky, started coming around once we got into our place. He saw his son for the first time at about the age of three. He cried the first time he looked at Mickis, and he said, "He looks like me." He would just stand in front of Mickis and watch him sleep. He would drive from Crossett after he got off work a few nights a week; Mickis would be asleep most of the time he got there.

He would purchase Pampers, milk, and clothing for his son at times. We would sit and talk about us and Mickis, but there was no attraction there anymore for him. He would drive from Crossett, which was about one hour and thirty-five minutes after work, now about three to four times a week to visit his son.

Then he would stay the night—in the other room because Mickis slept with me—and get up early in the morning, drive back to Crossett to work at GP (George Pacific, which was a paper company). This went on for about two months and a half. Then he asked me to marry him, but I told him no. I was not ready for that. Shortly after that, the visits became shorter, then he told me, if I didn't marry him, he didn't want his son either! I was so disappointed because he just came into Mickis's life. It was not about him and me, but his son's life. We never heard from him again.

A few years later, Ricky got married to someone else. When Mickis was about five and a half years old, he started asking questions about his dad. I never told my son anything negative about his father. I felt, in time, he would see for himself. Every year on Father's Day, I would encourage my son to call his father and wish him "Happy Father's Day." When Mickis was thirteen, he reached out to call his dad, Ricky, as he normally would do on Father's Day every year. Ricky's wife answered the phone, and Mickis asked if he could speak with his dad. She told Ricky, "Mickis is on the phone. He wants to speak with you!" Mickis's dad said to his wife, "Tell him I am not here." Mind you, Mickis could hear him saying this to her. What a blown *wow*. Mickis was so disappointed after that. He said, "Mom, please don't ask me to call him again." Ricky had not seen Mickis since he was around four. What a great disappointment! There was not much talk about Ricky after that disappointment.

ROSE HOGANS

Your thoughts:

ONGOING BEATINGS

This gentleman named Jeff was really a smooth talker and always appeared to be right there. Now Jeff, whom my dad would allow us to go places with, really started hanging around me after I got my place, and I didn't think too much about it. He was much older than me. He turned me on to marijuana, which I tried for two weeks. All his friends would gather at my house to smoke weed. One day as we were smoking weed, I happened to look over at my son as they were passing the joint around, and that day, I stopped and did not allow it anymore in my house because I did not want my son to see his mother using drugs and thinking it was okay.

So as time went on, I was around nineteen and a half, and the true personality of Jeff started coming out. He would start arguments about nothing, and it would snowball from there. He started accusing me of cheating and flirting with other guys, which I never did. I worked, went home, and took care of my son because my mom or my sister Lynda had him until I got home from work.

I can remember the first time Jeff hit me. We were fighting like cats and dogs. I was thinking to myself, *Surely this won't happen again, because he sees that I am not afraid of him.* A few days later, it happened again. We were fighting like cats and dogs again! The fights always started with him accusing me of something, then it would be that I was flirting or cheating.

The next night, the same thing happened. So I thought to myself, *Maybe if I don't fight him back, he would stop hitting me,* but it didn't work. Then every week for nine years, when he would start drinking, I would get beaten—he would drink almost daily! So the first couple of months, I thought, if I am just quiet and I didn't say anything back, the beatings would stop. They got worse. I don't remember three days going by when I was not cussed out, accused of something, or beaten.

I remember one weekend, getting beaten with a two-by-four for some hours. I turned black and blue with some black eyes from the beating. Then Jeff jumped on top of me and had sex. I had to wear makeup to cover up scars on my face; that's why I don't like makeup to this day. I always wore long sleeves to cover up bruises on my arms and turtlenecks for the choking bruises. I went each day not knowing what would set him off. He would drink and smoke daily and use pot. I would ask myself, How could someone be so angry all the time?

I remember a time we went to a club—which I didn't want to go to—when I stated I would like to stay home. I got punched, slapped, and made to go. Jeff started drinking, and as we were driving home, he started cussing me out and calling me names, saying this man looked at me. I got accused of giving him attention, and I didn't know what Jeff was talking about. I didn't see what he saw. I got pulled out of the vehicle, onto the pavement. He dragged me by my hair, pulling me down the street. My skin was burning. I was begging him, "Please stop, you're hurting me," but he would not listen to me. Jeff said, "I'm going to make you pay for someone looking at you."

After he finished dragging me, he started punching me, calling me all kinds of names. Then we got back to my place, and he jumped on me to have sex.

What a horrible feeling! I got beaten about everything. It got to the point I was afraid of Jeff and didn't know how to get out. He would be sweet one minute then, the next minute, so evil and abusive. After every beating came some type of sex.

My self-esteem was shot because of all the ugly things he would say to me, like I would never amount to anything, nobody wanted me, I was like dirt under his foot, he could treat me any kind of way and get away with it, and he would kill me before he allowed me to be with someone else.

I was so stressed out that I became numb to life and the beating. Every day, I heard more and more negativity.

I can remember a time when someone came to my door, looking for my sister. He heard the guy ask for her by name. I could see it already coming. When the guy left my door, he backhanded me, saying, "That guy was looking for you, but because he saw me here, he asked for your sister."

He got an iron skillet out of the kitchen and started beating me with it, saying, "Why do you make me do these things to you?" I got called all kinds of names—everything but a child of God. I have been beaten with guns, fish rods, wood, belts, hammers, pipes, broomsticks, tire rods, mops, pistols, extension cords, anything in reach, knives to my throat. He had threatened to slice my throat and throw my body in the woods. There were times he would just take scissors and cut my hair in different places (I always had pretty long hair), so I had to cut it short to make it even. He would call me all kinds of ugly names. I couldn't gain weight; I never smiled. I thought about killing myself so many times if I had to continue to live life this way. What kept me going was knowing I had a son who needed his mother, and I needed my son also. My thoughts would always go to my handsome son, and that would give me hope to live.

There were times I thought about killing Jeff; I did have a gun and knew how to use it, but I didn't want this man's blood on my hands or conscience. Isn't that crazy? *Wow*, to think that way when I was getting beaten literally to death every few days or weekly.

Another time Jeff took me out into the woods, beating me with big stumps of wood, dropping them on top of me, saying, "Don't you know I could kill you out here and no one will find you?"

It was seeing my son's face that kept me going. That night, Jeff broke my arm and then had sex with me. The next day, I could not move. Someone got me help. They took me to the hospital, where I stayed for a week. My body was banged up really bad, also with the bones in my arm being broken in many places because I always used my arms to shield my face. I wanted to press charges against him, but I was so afraid because I could hear his voice telling me, "I will kill you if you turned me in."

Somehow, he got into the hospital, apologizing, saying it won't happen again, blah, blah, blah. The police told me to kill him; nothing would happen to me. They acted like they were afraid of him!

When I got released from the hospital, I went to stay at my parents' house for a little while because my arm was broken and was put in a long cast. Jeff was always watching my parents' house when I was there.

One night, Jeff saw my dad leaving home, and he and a friend broke the door in, looking for me. He slammed my mom's hand in a drawer because she was reaching to get a gun to shoot him, then he turned around and slapped her. He dragged me out of my mother's house by my hair, pulled me to his truck, took me down the street, and beat me with a fishing rod and a shotgun, with a cast on my arm—so heartless. When my father came home, he did nothing after my mother told him what happened. My dad always looked the other way.

I was like a zombie walking around, but I had something to hold on to, which was my son. Each act of cruelty ended with sex of some kind until Jeff got finished. I was at the point in which I felt no one wanted me. I felt worthless, unattractive, and beaten down so badly. Still went to work almost daily, put on some type of makeup or long sleeves to cover the bruises, and wore a smile because I still had to take care of myself and my son. That was where I got some peace—being at work and with my son when I was home—because Jeff worked somewhere else.

I always had to tell him every detail of my day, and I had to repeat it to see if I said the same thing twice. If I didn't, I got beaten and called a liar and other chosen unpleasant words.

Many times, he would check my underwear, on a normal basis, to make sure there were no stains in them. If he thought there was, I got accused of cheating then slapped and beaten. He would check the miles on my car each day, making sure I didn't go anywhere after he would leave my house; he would pop up anytime at night. Jeff would be in the back of my house, looking through a window at night, seeing if I had anyone in the house.

I remember another beating with a fishing rod, getting hooked in the eye with a bass hook. A bass hook has many points on it. He wanted to just snatch it out of my eye. Thank God I still have my eye. He was so heartless and cruel.

I would pray so much, "Lord, please deliver me!" I used to journal a lot, expressing to the Lord how I felt. I was always accused of writing to some man because he would be in the window, watching me write when I thought he had gone home. I asked the Lord how much more could I take?

I was broken, depleted, feeling worthless, and I could not gain weight, had no self-esteem, always felt I was less than anyone else, was very quiet and withdrawn.

I remember Jeff and some of his friends going fishing, gigging fish late at night because the fish flowed to the top of the water at nighttime. So all you would have to do was stab them. That Saturday evening, they had been drinking and feeling no pain. They decided to get in a boat at midnight and go fishing. Jeff took me out there; I begged him to let me stay home. I can't swim. So I got cursed out and slapped a few times for not wanting to go. So in the boat we went. Jeff was at the front, standing up with the spear in his hand to stab the fish. The next guy in the second seat was the person holding the spotlight; then I was on the third seat, just there; then there was the guy controlling the boat, with the motor in the back. We were coming up to this tree in the river, and a snake was lying on one of the branches. Jeff was standing in the front, saying, "Turn the boat, turn the boat." The guy controlling the boat didn't hear him, so Jeff jumped into the river, then the next guy jumped into the river. The light was out; it was pitch black out there, and there was all this water. We didn't know where the snake went, and the guy on the back stood up. I begged him, "Please sit down. I can't swim." He turned the boat over, and I fell into the river (remember, I can't swim). So I went down one time somehow. I came up, then I went down again, and somehow, I came back up the second time. I screamed out, "Somebody, please help me!" I remember going down the third time. I saw a white shadow (which I knew was an angel) come and push me back up, then Jeff heard me scream and came back and grabbed me. I was so scared, I think I shook for days.

A few days later, the beatings started again because I didn't want to go deer hunting. I got beaten and pistol-whipped for that. I remember times when I could just be sitting, minding my business, and he would just haul off and hit me. We would go places I didn't want to go; he would say, "You sit in this corner like a good little dog, and you might not get beat tonight." I never was a drinker or smoker (except the two weeks I smoked weed) because of what I saw it was doing to the people around me. I always wanted to be in my right mind because I was scared straight enough with what I was dealing with daily!

Another time, Jeff put a gun to my head and said, "Do you know I could kill you right now?" He pulled the trigger, my life flashed before me, the gun just snapped. Jeff went to the next person and pointed it at their neck and shot them. He said he didn't put any bullets in the gun. Thank God, the person lived; the doctors said it was a clean shot. Jeff was crazy, and I was really afraid because he always threatened to kill me.

Another time; we started shooting pool just for fun, and there came a time Jeff would hustle people for their money. He would put me up to play against these people; he would bet them hundreds of dollars that I would beat them shooting pool. There were a few times I lose; did I pay for it with a pool-stick beating or worse. I became a great pool player through all this. He was happy when he had a pocketful of money at my expense. Wow, I was just thinking about my life and not getting beaten that night! I was a nervous wreck, wondering each day if I would live or die. Then as time went on, I purchased some land, about two acres, for $1,500. I paid cash for it. I paid to have it cleaned off and purchased a mobile home with three bed-rooms, with $500 down. Thank you, Jesus.

I think the payment was about $225 a month. At this time, I was working two jobs—one early morning at a little store, making donuts (real donuts from scratch) and frying chicken. I worked there from 4:00 a.m. until 1:00 p.m. then worked at Masonite Flooring Company from 2:00 p.m. until 10:00 p.m.

My only regret was leaving my son for so long with my parents every day. But the beatings slowed down because I worked most of the time throughout the week. It appeared I got beaten more on the weekend during that time. I thank God that He truly had His hand on me during this horrible time of my life.

If this, was you, what would you have done?

LAID OFF WORK

I worked both of these jobs for about two years. The convenience store went out of business because the owner died. About the following year, Masonite, the flooring company, closed its doors. I started drawing unemployment, but it was not enough to make ends meet, and I was used to having money to pay my bills and purchase things for my son.

I started bootlegging to make money, which was selling beer, Boone's Farm, 20/20, and different brands of wine, and hard liquor because we lived in a dry county, which was taking a risk. I could have gone to jail. To God be the glory, He had His hands upon me even in my sin. The business was great because most of the men came to me to get their beverages. Jeff would take my money, and for this reason, I always had some money hidden somewhere in the house. He never got it all as he thought! I always made sure I had money to pay my bills because he never helped me pay a bill at all; he always took money from me.

Jeff was always somewhere watching who came to my house, and I was still getting beaten through it all. As time went by, my hair grew back, and he would take scissors just to cut anywhere in my hair and cut on my arms also. So I had to constantly get my hair cut shorter or wear baseball caps because it was so uneven most of the time, then I would get cursed out because I cut my hair.

I am so glad I never got pregnant by Jeff because he would always throw away my birth-control pills. Mickis is my one and only child, whom God gave me!

I remember my son going to my father around the age of eight or nine, asking him, "If I killed this man, what would happen to me? I am tired of him beating my mom." You would think my dad would step up to the plate with his grandson going to him, saying something like that! But my dad would always look the other way, and he was still beating my mother. I never considered what my son was going through because I was just trying to survive.

So many times, I wish my dad would have protected me or just been there for me, but he never was; he always looked the other way. I never remember my parents ever telling me they loved me!

All I heard from my dad was how disappointed he was in me and always accusing both of my sisters of being like me, pregnant at a young age. But they both went on to finish high school. Thank you, Jesus.

So at around twenty-seven, I started thinking of ways to get out of Arkansas because this was affecting my son, even contemplated ways to kill Jeff.

About three weeks later, my sister Lynda and her husband drove to Arkansas. Their plan was to slip into town, kill Jeff, throw his body in the river, and leave before anyone saw them. But my little sister, Gwen, saw them and told my father. He jumped into his car and went after them. Lynda knew of some of the beatings but was not fully aware of all of what I was going through.

She went into the USMC right out of high school (thank you, Jesus). Jeff was always top-notch when others would come around, making it appear that he loved me! Yeah, right.

So while Lynda and her husband were at my house one evening, Lynda's husband came out of the bathroom from taking a shower, with a towel wrapped around him. I could see the expression of anger on Jeff's face. I knew it was going to be trouble for me. A few days later, after they left, going back to California, I got beaten for Lynda's husband coming out of the bathroom with a towel wrapped around him. That beating went on for some days! Jeff beat me so badly, I could barely walk. My face was swollen from the repeated slapping and punching, kicking, and stomping on my head.

I had to get to a phone. I never had one because Jeff would always be afraid I would try to get help. So after he left my house one night after beating and sex, I walked a little bit in so much pain (scared to drive my car because he always checked my miles) to use a neighbor's phone to call my sister Lynda. They had just walked into their home in California from the long drive from Arkansas. As soon as she answered, she heard me crying, and she said, "Jeff beat you again?"

"Yes, I need help, I have to get out of here!"

She said, "I am on the way." She jumped on the next flight, coming back to Arkansas. She did not give me time to change my mind, which I thank God for. So my sister rented a U-Haul and parked it somewhere out of sight for two days. At night we would fill it up with my belongings, and we left two days later in the middle of the night. I left my car, my guns, and my home. I didn't care what my mom did with it; I just had to get away!

This is not all my story about abuse; this is some of it. It would take a whole book to tell of all the nine years I encountered. There is so much more I could say about the sick, twisted things he did to me. He would urinate on my body. He would do things with bananas and cucumbers and more. The handle of knives and guns, also cut me on my arms and legs. He would kick and stomp me, as if he were kicking an animal. Jeff bit my nipples so hard until they would bleed and be numb. I don't want to get any more graphics than this. It's because of the grace of God I lived through this terrible time of my life.

It's the middle of the night, everything that I was taking with me was packed (without any help from my dad, how sad)! We kissed my mom and my little sister Gwen goodbye. Me, Lynda, and Mickis were in the U-Haul leaving to drive to California, which would take us about three or four days.

It took us about three days to get to California. We stopped for gas, food, and restroom breaks, then back on the road. This was a whole new world for me. This was the third time I left. One time after I recovered from one of the bad beatings, I left and went to stay with Lynda in South Carolina where she was stationed for the marine corps for about three weeks. I allowed Jeff to talk me into coming back home—*stupid* me!

Somehow, Jeff would always mysteriously get the phone number and contact me obsessively. Then the lies would start—"Give me another chance," "I am so sorry," etc. Blah, blah, blah. I believed him. Remember I'm a country girl who has never been anywhere, so sheltered from the real world and not knowing anything.

Another time, my son and I went to Chicago to stay with my aunt Ruby for a few weeks, but my aunt had her own situations going on. I didn't want to add more on her with me and my son. So of course, I went back to Arkansas with more beatings!

To top it all off, this *man was married! Please, before anyone judges me* or looks down on me and says "I would not have put up with this" or "I can't believe she messed with a married man!" remember my dad would not allow me to go anywhere unless it was with Jeff of whom I became afraid of. Never judge a book by its cover until you know the whole facts.

I tell you, if a man hits you once, he will do it again. Don't believe the lies when he says it will not happen again. *Please get out.* Your life depends on it! I have nine years of physical, emotional, sexual, and mental bruises and scars to show for it. I have knots in my head, scars on my back, bruises on my legs, scars on my eyes, and scars on my butt cheeks. These bruises and scars are visible, but the hardest ones are on the inside, which many haven't seen—low to no self-esteem; hearing negative things; dealing with feeling worthless, unattractive, uneducated, broken and being called stupid, ugly; always being accused of something; and much more.

I have a God who said, "Daughter, I will take your *scars* and turn them into *stars*." It is through the grace of God that I am alive to tell my story. I have never saw a good example of love; all I have ever witnessed were abuse, alcohol, smoking, lying, cursing, cheating, and gambling. I could never remember being told "I love you" by anyone, not even my parents! I moved out of my parents' house and got into the same type of situation and abuse my mother was in. So I did my best to show my son, Mickis, the love I never knew. Jesus is still teaching me how to love him and how to love myself.

Now, listen to me. I love you and say to myself and to you, "We are winners." We are overcomers, we are healed, and we are whole. We are somebody! We can do anything with and through the help of the Lord!

Penny for your thoughts

NEW BEGINNINGS

We were in California now, living with my sister Lynda and her son, learning a whole new way of life. I would have to say to myself out loud *"caged no more"* over and over the first three months I was there in California. I had to convince myself because I would dream of Jeff being on top of me, beating me to death. Lynda would go into my room quite often and gently wake me from the nightmare, after which I was shaking and crying. When I would awaken, I was grateful it was just a dream. *Was I free?*

I enrolled Mickis in school after about a few weeks of being in California. He was in the fourth grade, and I started working on the marine corps base at one of the banks as a bank teller, learning the swing of things, within 2 months. About eleven months later, Lynda got orders!

She had to leave within a few months. She got stationed overseas for a year. She had a two-year-old son, and I was scared to death that my security blanket was leaving me!

So she taught me how to get around—drive from our apartment in Santa Ana to the school and the base and grocery stores. She did most of the driving because it was too fast-paced for me.

Things appeared to be looking up, or so I thought! I learned my way around, and I felt I could do this. So it was just me, my son, and my two-year-old nephew Chauncey.

Men would try to talk to me, but I gave no one the time of day for about two years—still trying to learn how to gain self-esteem, letting go of being worthless and feeling unattractive, and learning the fast pace of California!

So one day, I got home from work, the phone rang, and it was Jeff from Arkansas. I started trembling, so this let me know I was not set free just to hear his voice. *I cringed, and fear gripped me.* Of course, he started to sweet-talk me, asking why I left. He kept apologizing, which was like blah, blah, blah. I kept saying to him, "Why don't you be a husband to your wife? I already feel bad for the nine years I was in your life. Your wife didn't deserve what I did to her!"

So every day, he would call once, twice, or three times a day. I got to the point, some months later, I told Jeff, "Just send me the money, I will come back," which was a lie. I was not planning to move back to Arkansas at all. I was just trying to get back some of the money that was taken from me those nine years.

So after about six months of him sending me money, he decided to come to California. My mother called me and told me Jeff was flying to California! I was scared to death. Jeff had my address because he was sending me money. So I packed up some clothes, took my son and my nephew, left home for about three days, and went to stay with a girlfriend!

I was so afraid, but I kept telling myself, "You're not in Arkansas anymore. He can't hurt you." I kept Mickis out of school for about three days, taught him how to get to the police station, which was not too far from our apartment.

After the third day, I felt sorry for Jeff, knowing he was camped outside my apartment because he kept leaving messages thirty to forty times a day on my phone, which I could check from anywhere. I felt bad because Jeff was sleeping in front of the apartment building the whole time I was at my girlfriend's house. The only thing he knew was my address. So I picked him up on the fourth day, but I kept my son close. Jeff started to fuss at me, saying, "Why did you let me stay out here for three days?" I didn't open my mouth. I just looked at him.

I allowed Jeff to take a shower and sleep in the other room. My son and my nephew slept with me. I told Jeff he needed to prepare to go back to Arkansas. There was nothing here for him. Jeff brought a ring to ask me to marry him—*wow*. But remember, he was already married! So the next day, we were all out, and we got a bus ticket for Jeff to go back to Arkansas and a bit to eat. My uncle Joe, who lived in Los Angeles, about forty to fifty minutes away, got a call from someone in Arkansas, letting him know the guy Jeff who was beating me came to California. My uncle Joe said, "I got this! This is my niece. No one will ever hit her again, not on my watch!" So that day (as I heard later), my uncle Joe kept drinking gin. He got his .45-caliber pistol and went to my apartment in Santa Ana. We were not there—thank God—because he drove from Los Angeles to my apartment in Santa Ana to kill. He sat there in front of the door of my apartment, for about two and a half hours. Every time the elevator door opened down the hall from my apartment, he was ready to shoot. God knows best! I found out about it a few days later, by which time Jeff had left and gone back to Arkansas. Once Jeff got back to Arkansas, he kept calling for about a few months, then the calls stopped after he saw I was done with him. I felt so much better and relieved to go on with my everyday life.

Still not free. The dreams started again for about a few months, then they started slowing down. I always kept my son close. So as time went by, I got better, and I started branching out; going to the e-club, the gym, and the car wash; and moving around town, hanging out with my girlfriends. I still worked on my self-esteem. The bank went out of business, and I start working at the commissary (which is the grocery store for the military families). I started meeting new friends but was still not ready to get into a relationship with anyone yet.

This was about the third year being in California. I would go to the car wash weekly, and this gentleman always seemed to be there. He would always speak to me, and then he started offering to wash my car. The first few times, I said, "No, thanks, I got it." He was very persistent, then we started to talk a little.

He was very complimentary, which I was not used to, telling me how pretty I was, how he liked my smile, etc. I still had to work within myself to believe it. He would start helping me wash my car. I would look at this man and say "Man, he is fine," but I wouldn't tell him. I just said it to myself, thinking this man would not want me! An unattractive, broken country girl like me!

Then he asked me out to dinner the first few times. I made excuses and said no. Then I asked myself, "What would be the harm?" So we went to dinner, then more dinners, then to clubs. I never drank or smoked. I just loved to dance, and I started going to work out at the gym, etc. He made me laugh, and we had great conversations; we spent lots of time together. He was a Marine, very good-looking, built, and fine. He was so gentle, patient, and kind. He pursued me for over a year, then I gave in, and we became friends with benefits—*wow*—but he was married. So after about a year and a half, I started falling for him, so I had to break it off. I cried, and he cried also, but I knew it wasn't right seeing this married man. He belonged to someone else, and I wanted him for myself! So we just remained friends (without benefits). We are still friends to this day. Yes, it was very hard because I never had a gentleman like him.

Shortly after, my mother and little sister Gwen came to California to get away from my dad, who was still abusing her. My mother was taking a bath one night, and I offered to wash her back and saw bruises up and down—both her arms and her back. I wanted to cry. Mind you, my dad had been abusing my mother for as long as I could remember, starting at the time I was around four years old.

She was doing so much better in California. She got a job at the day care my nephew went to on base. She also met a friend, and she spent time with him quite often at his place at the apartment complex we lived in. We were happy to see her smiling again. They stayed with us about eight months before she allowed my dad to persuade her to go back home to Arkansas. We begged her not to go back, to stay with us, but she kept saying "Charlie needs me." So back to Arkansas they went—her and Gwen—and the abuse started again.

My sister Lynda came back to California from Japan. She got stationed at Marine Corp Base Camp Pendleton. She offered for me and my son to move with her into base housing at Camp Pendleton, which was a blessing, but I decided to stay at my job on the base. My son, Mickis, and I moved to Irvine, California. He was going into the seventh or eighth grade in middle school.

I was still working at the commissary but, a few months later, started working at another bank as a proof operation on the Marine Corp Base. A friend introduced me to her friend, about a year after I broke it off with the married guy I met at the car wash. This guy was a Marine also but later became a police officer, and no, he was not married— thank You, Jesus. We started dating and never really became friends. We dated for about two years, with many ups and downs. He was always busy, as he would tell me!

But I remember one night, going over to Ben's apartment and knocking on his door. He did not want to let me in, which was strange, so Ben started making excuses to keep me outside, but when he opened the door, I pushed past him and went into the apartment. I asked him, "Are you hiding something?" Then I walked into his bedroom. There was a female lying in his bed—*wow*. He kept apologizing. "Rose, I did not want you to see that." But how unfair! Ben had the freedom to come to my apartment any-time—day or night—and I thought I could do the same! I was committed to the relationship.

We never did a lot of things together because he was always working (*well*). The thing we lacked most was communication. Now, remember I never had a real relationship or friendship with anyone except the married guy before him, at this point in my life! Still wanting us to work, I was there anytime Ben needed me to help him or do things for him. But I didn't fully trust him after seeing that lady in his bed!

My little sister, Gwen, kept asking my dad if she could come to visit us in California during the summer, but he kept making excuses and wouldn't allow her to come. So when she graduated from high school (which was within six months), I sent her a plane ticket, and she came to live with us.

I got a new job off the base, working at a bank as a bank teller, making more money. The police officer and I still saw each other off and on, mostly booty calls. I cared about him and was looking forward to seeing where this would go.

My sisters would get so upset with me for helping Ben all the time. They would say, "He is just using you!" They were right, but I always tried to see the good in everybody, and I wanted to experience love—still trying to learn about myself, be a mother and sister, also work a full-time job—and see Ben when he had time for me! I always knew there has to be better! I started seeing life differently. There was a void in my life!

Notes

YEARNING FOR
MORE IN LIFE

I started losing interest in clubbing, hanging out with friends, and even Ben, the guy I was seeing. I was drawn to learn more about Jesus. I started going here and there, in search of a church home. Now I am praying to God for a church home where I could be fed the truth.

About a week later, I met a gentleman named Clay, whom my girlfriend Brenda introduced me to. Her husband and Clay were coming from being stationed in Japan, which they both were in the USMC. Clay and I became amazing friends. He was so different from any other gentlemen I had known. When Clay would talk with me, he always included Jesus in the conversations, and he walked what he talked, which made me want to hear more about Jesus. Clay witnessed to me about Jesus and talked about the baptism in Jesus's name and about speaking in tongues as God gives the utterances.

He patiently shared Scriptures to back up what he said.

Peter replied, "Repent and be baptized,
every one of you, in the name of Jesus Christ
for the forgiveness of your sins. And you will

receive the gift of the Holy Spirit. The promise is for you and your children and for all who are far off—for all whom the Lord our God will call." With many other words he warned them; and he pleaded with them, "Save yourselves from this corrupt generation." (Acts 2:38–40 NIV)

Very well then, with foreign lips and strange tongues God will speak to this people, to whom he said, "This is the resting place let the weary rest"; and, "This is the place of repose"—but they would not listen. (Isaiah 28:11–12 NIV)

When the day of Pentecost came, they were all together in one place. Suddenly a sound like the blowing of a violent wind came from heaven and filled the whole house where they were sitting. They saw what seemed to be tongues of fire that separated and came to rest on each of them. All of them were filled with the Holy Spirit and began to speak in other tongues as the Spirit enabled them. (Acts 2:1–4 NIV)

There was a man of the Pharisees, named Nicodemus, a ruler of the Jews: The same came to Jesus by night, and said unto him, Rabbi, we know that thou art a teacher come from God: for no man can do these miracles that thou doest, except God be with him. Jesus answered and said unto him, Verily, verily, I say unto thee, Except a man be born again, he cannot see the kingdom of God. Nicodemus saith unto him, How can a man be born when he is old? Can he enter the second time into his mother's womb, and be born? Jesus answered, Verily, verily, I say unto thee, Except a man be born of the water and of the Spirit, he cannot enter into the kingdom of God. (John 3:1–5 KJV)

And afterward, I will pour out my Spirit on all people. Your sons and daughters will prophesy, your old men will dream dreams, your young men will see visions. Even on my servants, both men and women, I will pour out my Spirit in those days. (Joel 2:28–29 NIV)

Now when the apostles which were at Jerusalem heard that Samaria had received the word of God, they sent unto them Peter and John: who, when they were come down, prayed for them, that they might receive the Holy Ghost: (for as yet he was fallen upon none of them: only they were baptized in the name of the Lord Jesus). Then laid they their hands on them, and they received the Holy Ghost. (Acts 8:14–17 KJV)

While Peter was still speaking these words, the Holy Spirit came on all who heard the message. The circumcised believers who had come with Peter were astonished that the gift of the Holy Spirit had been poured out even on the Gentiles. For they heard them speaking in tongues and praising God. (Acts 10:44–46 NIV)

Clay took time to teach me the scriptures. One evening, my friend Brenda, her husband, and Clay came over to my apartment. We were just sitting around, talking about Jesus. I jumped up and said, "Okay, I believe. What do I need to do to be saved? I want this." So right in my living room, they prayed with me and over me and told me to say "thank You, Jesus" over and over again and sometimes saying "hallelujah." This is the highest praise we could give God. They kept saying, "If you think of Him, you would thank Him. You are just telling Him 'Thank You' for all the wonderful things He has done for you." Within a little while, I heard words that were not English coming out of my mouth. I saw something, like a ball of light, coming down upon me. I remember as if it were yesterday. It was May 16, 1990. I received the Holy Ghost, with the evidence of speaking in tongues, right there in my apartment. But remember I spoke in tongues when I was thirteen.

My girlfriend Brenda attended a church in Oceanside, California, where I would go with her occasionally, but I was feeling there was more for me. I thanked God for using Clay, coming back from being stationed in Japan. He invited me to his church; he attended Peace Apostolic in Los Angeles. I felt the presence of God and that place, in people were so free and friendly.

I came home so fulfilled from listening to the word of God being taught there. So I prayed to seek God's face about this place for me to fellowship. I heard, "This is it, home fellowship, here!"

Clay and I became the best of friends. We did everything together. We went to church together, movies, dinners, walking, etc. One of us would cook one day, and the other would do so the next day, depending on our work schedules. He was still in the USMC. We would, at times, call each other at 2:00 or 3:00 a.m., get up if one of us was hungry, go to eat at Denny's, and laugh and talk. We studied the Bible together, and we called each other all the time. Everyone assumed we were dating because we spent so much time together. We would ride together, pray, cry— we did everything together as amazing friends. He would get my advice about different women, and I would get his advice about Ben, whom I was still seeing. We would talk for hours. If there were times one of us didn't have money, we took care of each other—my ride-or-die friend—but there was no spark there at all for either of us. I remember that we kissed one time just to see if there was a spark— nothing but an amazing friendship.

One morning, at about 3:00 a.m. Clay called me, crying that his mother had passed. I hurried up, got dressed, and went to his house. What a sad time. We just cried together. I offered to go with him to his hometown, but he said, "I will be okay." So I drove him to the airport early the next morning. After I dropped him off at the airport, my two sisters and I went to *The Price Is Right* taping. We were not too far from there by the airport. We got on the show. I got picked to go on stage to win a prize. (I won a grandfather clock to get on stage, which I gave to my mother.) We had a great time. A week later, Clay comes back from the funeral.

One evening, Clay was driving me home after having dinner at his place. We saw this guy crossing the street, right by the railroad tracks (which was close to my apartment). The guy was naked. Clay looked at me, and I looked at him. Did we just see—what we thought—was a naked person? I told Clay, "Let's go help the guy." We parked at my apartment. I went upstairs and got one of my son's T-shirts and a pair of shorts.

My friend, Clay, went to the guy and helped him put the clothing on. So I told Clay, "Let's take the gentleman upstairs to my apartment and feed him." This man had burn marks all over his arms and legs (they look like cigarette burns) and hair like an Afro. We tried to talk with him, but he just stared at us. I fixed a plate of food for him, put it in front of him, but he would not eat it. So we called the paramedics, and they came and took him somewhere.

After everything was done, I asked Clay, "Do you think we just entertained an angel without knowing it?" ("*Do not forget to entertain strangers, for by so doing some people have entertained angels without knowing it*" [Hebrews 13:2 NIV].). "Do you think we were being tested? If so, I hope and pray we pass the test by clothing him and trying to feed him." Then I heard, "Whatever you did for one of the least of them, you did for me" ("*The king will reply Truly I tell you, whatever you did for one of the least of these brothers and sisters of mine, you did for me*" [Matthew 25:40 NIV].). We experienced many amazing things together, watching Jesus work. My friend Clay and I are still amazing friends to this day. It's priceless!

I was still seeing the police officer. He went to church with me a few times, but it never sparked an interest for him as it did for me. I could remember him still coming over some nights after he got off work and spending the night with me, but I would not have sex with him because my mind was on learning about Jesus.

I remember, one day, the Lord told me to stop playing with this man's heart, "Either it's going to be Me or him." So I broke it off with him. *No ringy, no dingee!* We are still friends. It was hard because I really cared about Ben, but I was looking for love in all the wrong places. Now I am learning to love Jesus, and He is teaching me about true love. *Ben was better than what I ever had!* I thought.

Now I was in church for about six months and loving it, not seeing anyone, just learning, stretching, and growing into who God wants me to be. Then I met this gentleman by the name of Ted, who would go in the bank quite often and wait in line until my window would open, then we would do his transactions. Ted would flirt a little bit and talk about church, telling me he was a minister. Ted would come to the bank three or four times a week, always waiting until my window was available. He finally asked me out to lunch, and he would always give me scriptures to read about Jesus: Acts 2:38–40 (NIV); John 3:1–5 (NIV); Acts 1:8 (NIV), "*But you will receive power when the Holy Spirit comes on you*"; Colossians 3:17 (NIV), "*And whatever you do, whether in word or deed, do it all in the name of the Lord Jesus*"; and Acts 4:12 (NIV), "*Salvation is found in no one else, for there is no other name under heaven given to men by which we must be saved.*"

So every time I saw Ted, we talked about the scriptures, and he explained them well. I would eagerly go home and read the scriptures he would give me for that day. Every day he came, he had new scriptures for me: Joel 2:28–29; 1 Corinthians 15:4 (NIV), "*That he was buried, that he was raised on the third day according to the Scriptures*"; Romans 6:1–2 (NIV), "*What shall we say, then? Shall we go on sinning so that grace may increase? By no means! We died to sin; how can we live in it any longer?*"; Romans 6:3–4; Romans 8:9 (NIV), "*You, however, are controlled not by the sinful nature but by the Spirit, if the Spirit of God lives in you. And if anyone does not have the Spirit of Christ, he does not belong to Christ*"; Romans 12:1–8; Romans 12:9–21; and more. Then Ted would explain to me the meaning if I didn't understand them. His knowledge of the word of God impressed me—being so new in learning the Scriptures!

Occasionally, he would come by my apartment. We would sit at the table and read scriptures. Then one day, I said, "I want to be baptized right now," in the name of

Jesus. We had a pool there in our complex. Ted said, "Just come to church with me on Sunday. We could baptize you there." My response to him was "Tomorrow is not promised to me. Let's do it right now." He baptized me, my son, and my sister Lynda that evening, in the name of Jesus. "*Never boast about tomorrow. You don't know what will happen between now and then*" (Proverbs 27:1 GNT). Coincidentally, my friend Clay and Ted went to the same church: Peace Apostolic in Los Angeles.

God used two different people to say the same thing; they did not even know each other! "*In the mouth of two or three witnesses shall every word be established*" (2 Corinthians 13:1 KJV).

As time went on, we started going to dinners and movies. So I thought, *It will be fine. This is a minister.* Ted was always the perfect gentleman. So one day, after dinner, he said, "I have to go by my hotel room."

I stated, "Okay, I will stay in the car while you conduct your business."

But he kept saying "Please just come up with me for a minute. I am meeting a client."

I kept saying "No, I don't think it's a good idea."

Ted kept pressing and pressing; I didn't have a good feeling about it, but I went up with him anyway, thinking he was meeting a client for business. When we got in the door, he snatched me on the bed. I was trying to push him off me, begging him, "Please stop! This is not right." Ted snatched my underwear off and did his business. Ted raped me!

This really threw me for a loop. We had never even kissed or talked about sex, and then this happened! I cried like a baby. "Please take me home." I felt so dirty and as if I were back in Arkansas again after that happened to me! I did not want to talk to him or see him anymore even when he would go to the bank. I didn't want to talk to him. I looked at him differently from that day forward. He kept apologizing. I accepted his apology, and I also asked him to forgive me if I did anything to make him treat me that way. I talked to the pastor at church about what happened to me; he set him down from being a minister.

I got rebaptized in Jesus's name and got a good refreshing of the Holy Ghost! I told myself, *This, too, shall pass.* With the help of the Lord, I got through it. I wrapped myself up in Jesus. I was in church every Sunday morning, every Sunday night, every Wednesday, and sometimes, even during Sunday school, I got churchy. I could not get enough of God's word. I would study every scripture my pastor would give us and listen to the Word as I slept at night.

I would think in my heart how God could take someone like me—so broken; so abused; beaten down; one with no education, no self-esteem, no confidence—and draw me out of such a horrible pit, teaching me real love and to trust him through it all.

For a lady like me who never finished high school, the Lord had allowed me to manage and run businesses, built up my confidence. I read this verse of Scripture over and over about confidence: "*So do not throw away your confidence; it will be richly rewarded. You need to persevere so that when you have done the will of God, you will receive what he has promised"* (<u>Hebrews 10:35–36</u> NIV). He taught me that I am valuable. He taught me great self-esteem and how to read His word with understanding and confidence. He loved me with all my flaws and drew me with cords of love. I am a rare jewel and a virtuous woman. He was teaching me how to trust Him and to give Him my hurts, pains, and disappointment—letting go of what or who is making me stop!

I had to be honest with myself; I have problems, and I need God's help! Take off the mask; <u>identify (1) </u>who or what is causing me pain/hurt, (2) what people (3) make changes (4) look at self; <u>talk about it</u>; take the skeletons out of the closet; and take the necessary steps to be healed.

Notes

LEARNING TO
BE SET FREE

The Lord started dealing with me about forgiveness and unforgiveness. So I started studying and searching the scriptures about that subject. I wanted to be obedient to everything He told me to do. So I asked the Lord, "Who do I need to forgive?" He told me, my dad, Charlie, first then Jeff who abused me and Ted who raped me, and I had to learn to forgive myself. That was the hardest for me. So I asked the Lord to open the door for me to forgive, and He did.

I called my dad first. I talked to him about the Lord, and he said it didn't take all that. I also let him know I forgave him for not being the father I needed and not being there to protect me from the abuse that I went through for all those years and watching him abuse my mother. He never once said "Forgive me," but I was free from that. Then I asked the Lord, "Who's next?" He told me it was Jeff who beat me for nine years. So I called him up to talk to him about the Lord first. I told him I forgave him for every time he beat me, every time he called me out my name, every time he put me down, and for the things he did to me sexually. I asked him to forgive me, and he did ask me to forgive him also—and I did.

I felt a lot better because a huge burden was lifted off my shoulder after I talked to Jeff. I could feel some type of relief, but I was not done yet. Then I asked the Lord, "Who is next?" The gentleman (Ted) who raped me. I saw him at church, and I asked him to forgive me. I told him I forgave him for what he did to me. He kept saying, "Please forgive me. I messed up violating you like that. I have no idea what came over me!"

Now as some days have passed, I prayed, asking the Lord, "Have I truly forgiven?" There was a long silence, and then I heard, "I need you to call the lady in Arkansas and ask her to forgive you for sleeping with her husband. If you want to be set free!" I just said, "No, Lord. That is embarrassing." Humiliation kicked in. "Lord, please help me." That was a hard pill for me to swallow.

As days went on, I had to do it because I wanted to please my God, and I wanted to be set free from that which was hindering me. So I prayed and made the phone call, and she just happened to answer the phone. I could not speak to her at first, then I told her who I was, and I asked her if she would please forgive me for everything I put her through. She told me she would not forgive me, but I did my part out of obedience to the Lord. Then I asked her once again if she could find it in her heart to forgive me. She said no and hung up on me. What a humbling experience. Now I felt some relief because I did what I was told to do, but I was still sad because I hurt her. I was still not done! I had to work on forgiving myself. So I got started digging out Scriptures.

> *For if ye forgive men their trespasses, your heavenly Father will also forgive you: But if ye forgive not men their trespasses, neither will your Father forgive your trespasses.* (Matthew 6:14–15 KJV)

> *Forbearing one another, and forgiving one another, if any man have a quarrel against any: even as Christ forgave you, so also do ye.* (Colossians 3:13 KJV)

> *Be kind and compassionate to one another, forgiving each other, just as in Christ God forgave you.* (Ephesians 4:32 NIV)

> *He does not punish us as we deserve or repay us according to our sins and wrongs._* (Psalm 103:10 GNT)

Who do you know who needs your forgiveness?

SCARS INTO STARS

The Lord told me, "I will show you how to work on you and your self-esteem. You are worthy, you are beautiful, you are talented, I will teach you things you never knew. I will teach you many things through My word and give you understanding," and he did! "You are born again. That's the best education anyone can have. As long as you trust Me, obey Me, and listen to Me, I will teach you many things and work through you! I will be your help up on your most holy faith. I'm turning your *scars* into *stars*. I will give you confidence like never before, just stay close to Me!" I would hear the Lord telling me, "*I love you*, and I will teach you about true love." I never remembered my parents ever telling me they loved me. So I was on the search for true love, not being wrapped up in a man!

So I started a love affair with *Jesus*.

He is the lover of my soul.

He is like none other;

the tears I cry are tears of joy,

He wraps His arms around me with such gentleness.

I know He has millions of other children, yet He makes me feel as if I were the only one.

He never sleeps or slumbers.

He always has time for me.

He is a lover like no other.

He is generous, thoughtful, sensitive, strong, consistent, faithful, true, and He always keeps His promises to me.

He is so forgiving, patient, and kind.

He has loved me with an everlasting love.

He loved me to death! When I was out there polluted in my own blood, He came by and picked me up and said, "Why die, My sweet daughter, when you could live!" I am so grateful for His mercy and grace.

When I feel lonely, weak, and sad,

He has a way of lifting me. He is my strength, and he makes me laugh.

He always has time to listen to me.

He never pushes me away!

He is so divine. I love You, Jesus, and He treats me as the sweetest Rose of Sharon!

I had been in church for about three years, not seeing anyone since the police-officer Ben, just loving and learning me some Jesus, and He is still teaching me how to love him more and more. There is no greater love than Jesus! I am a work in progress, but he teaches me daily how to please Him. Yes, I had a few guys trying to talk to me, but as soon as one crossed the line by touching me or trying to kiss me, he had to go. *Jesus only* until I got married.

I would spend hours just sitting in front of my fish tank, watching the fish swim back and forth, without a care in the world. I wondered how they could be so free. It was so peaceful watching them swimming back and forth, me thinking about the love of God.

My daily routine was work, church, and home. Maybe a basketball game, if my son's team was playing. My son used to say, "Mom, your life is so boring." To me, it wasn't. I just took the time to learn more and more about Jesus. Talking to Him, praying, reading, being so grateful He loved me and was teaching me so many wonderful things. I would take index cards and write verses of scriptures on them to study them throughout the day.

Between customers, I would speak the verse of scripture out loud to myself. Faith comes by hearing and hearing by the word of God. At lunchtime, I would go to my car and have Bible class by myself unless someone wanted to join me.

Freely you have received, freely give.
(Matthew 10:8 NIV)

About six months later, I started having Bible study in our apartment in Irvine, Orange County, California. We had it on a Thursday night because we still had church on Sunday and Wednesday at Peace Apostolic, which was about forty-five minutes away, if it was good traffic. We invited people to church, but they would say that was too far to drive to Los Angeles, and my car was too small to carry many who wanted to go. So we talked to the pastor about starting one in my apartment in Irvine. We had a few ministers to volunteer to come down once a week to teach.

(Thanks to each of you for your sacrifice.) Then one minister committed every Thursday to teach the Bible class.

God did some amazing things through that Thursday-night Bible class. People were repenting, getting baptized in Jesus's name at the pool there in the complex, and receiving the Holy Ghost in my bathroom, my kitchen, my bedroom, and in my son's room. The Bible class kept growing, and the Lord allowed us to feed everyone spiritually and naturally. We always had enough food. Thank you, Jesus! We had to move out of my apartment because it was too small to fit all the people who would come! We had the Bible class there in my apartment for about a year and a half. What an honor to be used for the glory of God and see people coming and hunger after righteousness!

ROSE HOGANS

Notes

WELFARE AND FOOD STAMPS

Because of the abuse that I had gone through all those nine years in Arkansas, I had a blood clot in my left upper leg close to my thigh, which started to grow out of my leg. It had gotten as big as the size of a grapefruit. It had become very painful, pushing on the nerves in my leg and thigh and still growing; so I had to have surgery to have it removed. I was not able to go back to work at the appointed time at the bank because my leg didn't heal properly. Because a nerve got cut that was wrapped around the blood clot, the doctors wouldn't release me to go back to work before the workers' comp ran out.

So I went on welfare (back then it was AFDC [Aid to Families with Dependent Children]), trusting God for the result! Things did not look so well through the natural eye, but God was working in the spiritual realm on our behalf.

I saw God do some amazing things; we still had Bible study. The Lord always made a way so that we were able to feed the people at the Bible Study naturally, and still have leftovers. Coming from a full salary, getting paid every two weeks to getting workers' comp then welfare of $490 a month plus food stamp (paper books at that time).

*"For I know the plans I have for you,"
declares the Lord, "plans to prosper you and
not to harm you, plans to give you hope and
a future."* (Jeremiah 29:11 NIV)

I had to hold on to this!

God never fails

MANY TESTIMONIES
I COULD REMEMBER

I could remember a time when my lights were shut off on the day of the Bible study and I was hoping I could make it a few more days to make the payment, believing God to make a way for money. We asked my downstairs neighbor if we could run an extension cord to have electricity for the Bible class that night. Nobody ever knew the lights were off except for me, my son, the neighbor downstairs, and the minister doing the Bible class. People still received the Holy Ghost in that apartment that night. We didn't have electricity for about three days. Every day and night, I thanked God for making it possible for us to have electricity back on. Someone paid the bill, and to this day, I still don't know who paid for it, but to God be the glory. On the third day, the lights came back on. I just praised God and thanked Him.

I could remember another time when my sister Lynda and I were reading the Bible in my room while my son and his friends were in the living room, watching basketball on TV. I remember saying out loud, "I would love to make my family a Thanksgiving dinner." At that next moment, there was a knock on the door. My son went to the door and opened it. There were bags of groceries there. My son jumped over the bags, ran down the stairs, and did not see anyone left or right. He came back and called me out of the room, "Mom, Mom, come see this. There was a turkey, a ham, all the trimmings for Thanksgiving dinner, at the door!" God is amazing. I just spoke the word, and He answered. I praised Him and thanked Him for hearing my call and prayer.

I could remember another time I got my electric bill, which was about $125. I prayed over it and asked the Lord to show me favor as I called to make arrangements because, remember, I was on welfare, making $490 a month. I called to explain I wanted to make arrangements, and the gentleman on the line said, "Ms. Brown, you only owe us a penny." I said, "Excuse me?" He said, "You only owe us one penny." I praised God like never before; even the gentleman on the phone said, "Praise Him. He deserves it."

I could remember another time, going to the grocery store and having very little finances. I prayed, before I got out of the car, for the Lord to stretch the money that I had to buy food for me, my son, and my little sister, Gwen, who had moved in with me by now from Arkansas. So as I was at the meat counter, looking for the cheapest I could find, I looked down, and there was a pack of pork chop for $1. It was a big family package that we could eat off of for a few days (thank You, Jesus). When I got to the car, I praised God for providing for us yet another day!

I could remember another time. We drove to church, about forty-fifty minutes away. I had no money except what I was putting in church for my tithes and offerings—

no gas, and the gas hand was on E. But I was determined to go to church, and my son kept saying "Mom, we have no gas." I kept telling him to trust God, that He would provide so we could make it to church on E. We had amazing anointed service, and as I was going around the offering plate, thanking God for having money to put in for my tithes and offering, someone put something into my dress pocket, and I thought it was just a piece of paper with scriptures on it. I didn't think too much about it.

As we were going out of church that night, my son reminded me, "Mom, we still have no gas." I put my hands in my pockets. Still determined, I said, "Son, God will provide." I felt something as I took my hands out of my pocket—it was a $100 bill! Thank You, Jesus! So I was able to fill my car with gas, took them to get some Popeye's chicken, and praised God all the way home, telling my son and little sister, Gwen, how important it was to always give God our first fruit!

I have seen God's hand and so many wonderful, amazing ways in our lives; no one can beat His giving, His provision, His protection, or His amazing love. Allow me to give you a few more testimonies.

I could remember my car being a brown Buick Skylark, running out of gas, trying to make it to the service station. My car shut off, miles from a gas station. It coasted up the hill, down the hill, and up the hill again and down until it stopped right in front of the gas pump! God, again I praised Him. It was like angels pushing the car all the way.

I could remember Christmas rolling around, and I prayed to the Lord before we left to go to Bible study. "I want my child and my little sister, Gwen, to have a wonderful Christmas. Please make a way for them." So we left for Bible class that Wednesday night. We came home to a real, beautiful Christmas tree, with all the trimmings at our door on the second floor, and still to this day, we do not know whom God touched to do this. But to God be the glory. A week or so later, a school adopted Mickis and Gwen. They had so many presents; it was overwhelming. God is amazing. Thank You, Lord, for hearing my prayers, and I praised Him.

I could remember my Buick Skylark, which was so old that the radiator had a hole in it. I had to stop and put water in the radiator every few miles; I couldn't afford to purchase a new one! I remember my son being so embarrassed about our car. I couldn't drive it to church anymore like that because it started overheating. So I started praying to ask God for a newer vehicle because I wanted to go to church. One day about a week later, I stepped out on faith and drove to a car lot (cars, yes), praying all the way, "Lord, if this is You, open the door for me to use this Buick as a trade-in because I had no money to put down as a down payment. I was bringing in $490 a month!"

About a block from the car lot, I stopped to fill up the radiator with water and prayed, asking the Lord to not allow the water to run out or overheat. Now at the car lot, I was walking around, praying, asking the Lord which car He had for me. Then I spotted this car, all the way in the back, a white Isuzu I-Mark 1989 with a black ragtop sunroof—the most beautiful thing I had ever seen. Then I heard the Lord say, "That's it. That one is for you." So I had the sales guy take that one out. It was clean, had very low miles, was in great condition, and it was a turbo stick shift (which I hadn't driven since I moved from Arkansas). The first car I ever purchased was the green 1972 Nova Vega, which was a stick shift. The sales guy tried to talk me into something else. I told them, "I want this one." I had no money to put down. I had my faith and that Buick, in which the Lord allowed the water to stay in and which didn't run hot when they started it up. They looked at my credit and my little income ($490 welfare), saying there was no way I would get this car, but I held on to my faith, believing God for a miracle. Needless to say, I drove home in my new white Isuzu I-Mark 1989 car with a black ragtop sunroof, thanking and praising God all the way home. What a blessing, from a 1979 Buick to a 1989 Isuzu I-Mark. My payments were about $225 a month.

I could remember when my son became a senior; he was a star basketball player. All his friends were getting these letterman jackets with all their names and achievements on them, but he knew I could not afford it, so he never asked. I knew he wanted a jacket also. But I knew who could do it, so I prayed and asked the Lord to make a way for him to have one. So a few days later, I went into this store that made the jackets for the school, just looking around, believing by faith that God would make a way for my son to have a letterman jacket. As I was talking to one of the sales clerks, I told her what I was looking for: the Woodbridge letterman jacket for my son. She said, "By the way, we have one that someone ordered but did not need."

In my heart, I thought, *Lord, I know I can't afford it, but You can show me favor.* And I asked, "What is the price?" I was thinking To myself "I have $50." She said, "Fifty dollars, and we will add his name and achievements for *free!*" God struck again. I was floating out of the store on cloud Jesus! I forgot to ask about the size of the jacket! The jacket was large, but my son needed an extralarge one, but I presented it to him anyway. He was happy; because he did not want to hurt my feelings, he wore it a couple of times, but the sleeves were too short!

Remember I was on welfare, bringing in $490 a month. My rent was $620; CPS, about $125 a month; my car payment, $225; car insurance, about $60; telephone bill, about $35; and my tithes and offerings, $50 a month. I was taking out $5 a month, putting it into a savings account, wanting to start a business someday. Looking at those figures, tell me, is God amazing and extremely good? Through the natural eye, all looked impossible. *But is anything too hard for God* (Jeremiah 32:27 NIV)?

Look at God; we never got evicted. We always had a roof over our heads. Yes, my electricity got disconnected once, and my car got repossessed, and within a week, God touched someone's heart to pay the payment for me, and the place that repossessed it brought it back to my house! Thank you, Jesus. We ate pork and beans, weenies, and Hamburger Helper, with lots of pinto beans and rice, but we thanked God for our food. I was praying to the Lord about starting a business to help bring in some extra income. So I started making photo albums, dolls' dresses, little wedding favors to put on the tables at wedding receptions, with the hot glue gun. That was short-lived, burning my hands up. Still not released from the doctors from leg surgery.

I could remember, shortly after, the Lord put on my heart to sell cars. Asking the Lord to show me how to sell cars, he showed me favor, and I had a dream about having an ad and the newspaper about selling cars. When I went to pay my car payment at the lot where I purchased my Isuzu (Kars yes), I spoke to the manager and asked if they would be interested in doing commission with me for every client I referred to them. Just thinking of ways to bring some income into my home, I was thinking they probably would do about $50 per car, but they said, "Sure, we will give you $300 for every car sold through you." I agreed, and I went home and prayed, trusting God for the results. I ran a little ad in a PennySaviour, which was a *free* advertisement for selling cars. Mind you, I never went to the car lot after running the ad. People just started calling me. The first week, someone called from my ad. I got all the information, called a salesperson at the car lot. The first car sold an extra $300 that week (thank You, Jesus). I took out tithes and offerings. The next week, I sold three cars (thank You, Jesus) and repeated the same thing. Each week, God increased the sales. I got up to $6,500 a week. God is amazing, just from a small ad, trusting Him for the results. This went on for about eight months. The Lord allowed me to make more than the sales representative at the car lot did. God showed me favor. Thank you, Jesus.

What an honor to give Him my first fruit of everything, along with my life. God is amazing; these are not stories someone told me. I experience them and much more myself.

I have such a love story about Jesus.

He is my everything.
He is my all and all.

He has taught me so much: I've seen angels, I have heard angels talking in my room, I have felt God's presence on many occasions, I have seen God do amazing things and labored at the altar with people tarrying for the Holy Ghost—standing in the gap, interceding for many through prayer, God sharing and showing me ways to encourage precious ones.

The Lord showed me things that would happen beforehand, and I watched them come to be!

Battled in the spiritual realm with evil forces trying to attack my son, I would wake up in the middle of the night and pray and anoint my apartment. When I would go into my son's room, I would see this evil black figure (evil spirit) lying on top of him, trying to kill him. I would go into my son's room, calling on the name of Jesus, pleading the blood of Jesus, and commanding that spirit to get out of my home, in Jesus's name. It would skip away, making screaming sounds. My son would wake up, saying, "Mom, something was trying to smother me." I wouldn't welcome a lot of things or people into my apartment for that very reason.

I could remember being in my closet, praying for hours, and listening so I could hear from God. Then one evening, my son, Mickis, and my sister Gwen came into the house looking for me but couldn't find me; they would say we had missed the Rapture! When I would go out of the closet, they would be relieved, thinking they had been left behind!

I could remember my little sister, Gwen, was dating this guy named Melvin, who came to the apartment, looking for her. She was not there; she was out with friends. I had just made myself a bowl of beans and corn bread, getting ready to enjoy my dinner, and listen to Pastor Swancy's video. When he came to the door and I told him she wasn't there, he asked if he could use the phone, so he went into the apartment to use it. After he left, a spirit of sickness came upon me. I crawled to the couch to lie down because I felt nauseated. When my son came home about ten minutes later, he looked at me and asked, "Mom, are you okay?" His next words were "Mom, it's a spiritual warfare!" I got him to bring me the anointed oil. I prayed over myself first, calling on the name of Jesus.

I felt this spirit lifting off me. My son went to use the phone. As he picked it up, I stopped him, and I took it out of his hands because I had not anointed it yet after Melvin, my sister's boyfriend, used it. Be careful with what spirits go into your dwelling place. They are real. That bad spirit tried to oppress me; it couldn't get in me because of the Holy Ghost, or Holy Spirit. I thank God for the Holy Ghost.

I could remember having $100 in my savings account. I wanted to start some type of business. I took that $100 out of my savings account, spread it on my bed, and prayed

to the Lord, asking Him to direct me on what type of business should I do where He would get the glory out of it.
The next day, I went downtown to the wholesale district,
driving and praying, asking the Lord to stretch this $100 to
purchase what would be profitable and useful to sell. So as I
was walking in and out of stores, looking, the Lord allowed
me to see leather organizers with paper and pen—that
would be perfect to use at church to take notes. I purchased
ten of them in different colors, for $10 each. I used one on
Sunday at church, and people started coming to me, asking
where I got that from and how much it was. I told them it
cost $19.99, and my business started—Rosesthings. Sold
out in twenty minutes (thank You, Jesus). More people
came, wanting one. Someone even purchased the one I
was using. I had $200. I took out tithes and offerings—I
had $175 left. I blessed it and thanked God for it. That
Monday, I went downtown again and purchased more—it
sold out the next Sunday again. I watched God grow it to
more and more, so I started adding more leather purses and
wallets for men.

I could remember another time when my son wanted
to go to someplace with his friends. I would not let him go
because I had a very bad feeling about it. He was so mad at
me that his eyes turned red. I got my anointed oil and laid
hands on him in the name of Jesus. Shortly after, he told
me that something came upon him that he wanted to kill
me. Not today, Satan!

I could remember my son wanted to go to a party. I
allowed him to make the choice, but I told him that the
Lord showed it would be dangerous there. He should not

go, but he went anyway. So I just got down and prayed for him, asking the Lord to cover him and his friends, keeping them from any hurt, harm, or danger! So within a few days, my son came to me and said, "Mom, there was a shooting at the party, and a few people got shot." Wow. I thank God for the warning and protection.

I could remember the Lord gave me a dream about Mickis teaching the gospel and me seeing a lot of people around him. The Lord told me I would see my son be an ordained pastor before I left this earth. He was around fifteen at this time.

Then we got a phone call shortly after from some lady in Indianapolis. She was telling me that the Lord showed her that my son would not play basketball and that he would teach the gospel. *Wow.* So I gave my son the phone for her to tell him. She did, and he was mad, saying, "No, I am not. I am going to play basketball. I will be the next Michael Jordan." So that night, he went out and walked on the railroad tracks, saying, "If I can't play basketball, I will kill myself." That night, the train never came, and that train came around the same time each night (thank You, Jesus). We had no idea who this lady was, calling us from Indianapolis, but God knew. I always kept in the back of my mind everything the Lord said. So as time went on, Mickis kept playing basketball as varsity all throughout high school, nineth to twelfth grade. I remember him making some shoes with blocks and putting tape around them to walk around to help him jump higher.

When he was in tenth grade, he was playing in a street tournament. He messed up one of his knees, coming down from a dunk shot. He had torn ligaments and broke something. He had to have surgery. He was determined to play basketball. He went to rehab about two and a half weeks after surgery. My son ate, slept, played basketball. All throughout the house, there was always basketball dribbling. He would watch videos (VHS on VCR) of basketball games.

On his junior year, he started varsity again as he always did from ninth grade and up. He was back in the swing of basketball, but his knee kept on swelling after every game. It would be as big as a balloon, and he had to go to the doctor's office to get fluid drained off his knee. The doctors drained at least three full tubes of fluid about once or twice a week with this very long needle each time we went in. But his life was basketball. He was one strong young man. Through all of this, he still wouldn't stop playing. So it was basketball games supporting my son. I didn't miss a game unless it was Bible-study night, Sunday morning, or too-far-away games. We were my son's greatest cheerleaders—my sisters and I.

He made it through high school with both knees messed up from playing basketball. He finished high school in 1995. He got a basketball and track scholarship to a college in Sacramento.

My son, Mickis, went off to college in September 1995. Mickis had always been with me. The day he left me was a very sad day for me, and my world was turned upside down. I cried for about two weeks straight because my baby was going so far away from me. I prayed, "Lord, please help me," and He did. It was like a part of me was taken away, because he had always been with me. I was happy for him because he was doing something great with his life, but that was my heart, and all his eighteen years, he was with me. I would spend hours praying on behalf of my son, asking God to keep him from any hurt, harm, or danger.

I could remember, when I would pray for my son, the Lord would show me Mickis being back in Irvine. Then another time, the Lord showed me he wouldn't play basketball in college. I would downplay it but always kept in my mind the things the Lord would show me.

My son broke his wrist before basketball season started at practice one day up in Sacramento. The doctors had to put screws in his wrists because someone fell on his arm (he heard his wrists snapped) while coming down from a dunk. He came home with this big cast on his arm. So after that semester, 1996, he came home to heal that summer. Then he went back the next semester. Basketball was never the same for him. Every time he played after that, he would be in so much pain from his knees or wrist. So in 1999, he came home from college for good.

Needless to say, on July 2006, I saw my son ordained to be a pastor (thank You, Jesus). There's so much more to tell about Jesus. I have seen God's hand in and on my life! I am still not dating or seeing anyone yet. This was the early part of 1995. My sister Gwen got married in 1992 to Melvin, who was in the USMC: And he attended Peace Apostolic also. They moved into their place. Gwen got pregnant about three months after they got married.

I started doing hair in my apartment in 1991 for about a year before my little sister, Gwen, got married. I love to make ladies feel good about themselves because I never had it for me. I had a nice clientele (thank You, Jesus). Every head and hair got prayed over.

I enrolled in cosmetology school to do hair and nails at the end of 1992. I was so proud because I didn't think I could go to school without finishing high school, but God has always made a way for me and has taken amazing care of me. About my four months into school, my sister Gwen got extremely sick. She was about five and a half months into her pregnancy. The doctors put her on bed rest until after the baby was born because she had complications that could have made her have the baby early. They would keep her in the hospital, until after the baby was born, to monitor her because she had a high-risk pregnancy.

I dropped out of school to take care of her so she wouldn't have to stay in the hospital. I would stay at her house during the day while her husband went to work, then in the evening, he would care for her, with lots of prayers and reading Bible stories, laying on of hands, and anointing her stomach. With every doctor's appointment came great results. (Thank you, Jesus. To you be the glory.) Their baby, Marquis, came out a healthy baby boy, November 8, 1993, full term. Thank You, Jesus.

Mickis was still in high school, working, and Gwen had her own place. I would visit Gwen daily to help with Marquis, and I would take Marquis home with me in the evening to give her a break. As a baby, Marquis would spend two to three days and nights with me a week. At the age of five to six months old, Marquis heard about Jesus so much that when I would say *hallelujah*, his arms would raise high.

There were times when Marquis would be asleep and hear *hallelujah*, his arms would raise in his sleep. We would sing praise songs to Marquis and read Bible stories. Marquis would hear Pastor Swancy playing all the time; Marquis was singing praise songs before he could talk clearly. What a joy to teach Marquis the love of Jesus at such a young age. *"Train up a child in the way he should go: and when he is old, he will not depart from it"* (Proverbs 22:6 KJV). Marquis would say, "I got sprout up in the word of God!"

My mother came to California for the second time in August of 1995 to get away from my dad again because of the abuse and to see her new grandson. He was about to turn two years old in November. So my mother moved in with Gwen and her husband to help Gwen out with Marquis. My mother was doing so much better. She laughed more and started attending church with us and learning to enjoy her life. My dad kept calling my mom, asking her when she was coming home because he needed her help!

Within three months of my mother being in California, Melvin got orders to Japan. They were scheduled to be there by May of 1996. They wanted to take my mother as a live-in nanny, but she kept making excuses to go back to Arkansas. She left the second week of December 1995 going back to Arkansas. We even tried to get my mother to move in with me. I was still single at this time. My dad kept calling almost daily, telling her he needed her. We literally begged her not to go back, but my father's pull was greater than us! They had been together for over thirty-five years. "Please, Mom, stay here in California if you don't want to go to Japan!" She came to church with us one more time that Sunday. That Sunday, our pastor had an altar call like never before. He was pleading with someone to get up before mercy runs out. Many people came forward for salvation, but he kept saying, "There's still one more. Please come. God is calling you."

My sisters and I were praying, hoping my mother would go forward, but she wouldn't. She kept saying, "I am not ready to give my life to the Lord." That Monday morning, my mother left going back to Arkansas. The first night she got home, the abuse started again!

ROSE HOGANS

Notes

BACK TO WORK

Now the doctors had released me to go back to work in June of 1995 after my leg surgery. The bank job was filled, so I went to work again at the commissary at Marine base as a cashier in June of 1995. I was still doing my business, Rosesthings, selling leather goods.

I had been in church for about five and a half years now. Mickis was in college, getting ready to come home. Gwen and her family were getting prepared to move to Japan. My sister Lynda and her son Chauncey were stationed at Marine Corps Base Camp Pendleton, Oceanside, California. Getting back into the swing of work, church, loving life, and learning to love me, I have no boyfriend yet, single and celibate, learning Jesus!

ROSE HOGANS

Notes

IS THIS MR. RIGHT?

One day in the latter part of October 1995, as I was at my register, ringing up groceries for the military families, this couple (as I thought) came through my line. I greeted them, as I always did to everyone. I started small-talking with them. Seeing they were purchasing pampers, baby formula, etc., I congratulated them on their new baby. The young lady said, "This is not my husband, he is my coworker." They both had on military uniforms. "He just came with me on our lunch break. My husband isn't in the service."

Then the gentleman with her smiled at me and said, "Hello."

My response back was "hello, sir."

He extended his hand to shake mine, then he said, "My name is Billy."

I said, "My name is Rose."

He said, "I am looking for a wife."

My response to that was "may the Lord bless you with one!"

Billy then asked, "*Are you married?*"

"No, I am not."

Then he asked, "May I have your number?"

I wrote it on the back of a receipt with my name, thinking nothing else about it. A few weeks went by, he called the evening of November 10, 1995. (I remember because it was Marine Corps' birthday.) We talked for about three to four hours on the phone that night. Billy had a deep voice like Barry White's, so I said to him, "You can clear your throat and talk in your normal voice now. Stop pretending to sound like Barry White."

He started to laugh and cleared his throat and started again with the same voice. I love a man with a deep voice. He didn't know that! Every day after that first phone call, we would talk on the phone for hours! We talked about everything. I started noticing him going into the commissary more, like daily coming through my line.

I started praying because I could see Billy starting to pursue me. In one of our phone conversations, Billy asked me, "What does a young lady like yourself do besides work?"

I told Billy, "I go to church a lot—Wednesday-night Bible study and Sunday morning and Sunday-night services." I thought Billy wouldn't be interested now. Billy asked if he could go with me to church on Sunday. I was so surprised! Now I really started to pray for the Lord's will to be done. Sunday came, and Billy picked me up for church. This was the first time we did anything together besides talking on the phone and me seeing him at the commissary.

One of my pacific prayers were "Lord, if this is the man for me, allow him to repent and be baptized in Jesus's name and also to receive the Holy Ghost with the evidence of speaking in tongues and desire to learn you more and more."

Billy started to go to church with me every week on Sunday and Wednesday. Now that impressed me to a point he would remind me about church—still talking on the phone, having dinners, and him still coming to the commissary when I worked!

Some of my other prayers were "Lord, if this is the man you have for me, allow him [whomever] to ask my father for my hand in marriage" also "When he walks into my presence, allow my heart to skip a beat and flutter!" I needed the word of God to back it up as things appeared to get serious with us, and as I started to like him, I would fast a few days a week, seeking answer from God!

Then my mind went to my son, Mickis. What was he going to think, and how would I tell him about Billy? Mickis was coming home from school in a few weeks! My son had always said to me, "Mom, I will not allow another man to hit you or hurt you again." I thought about the hurt and pain my son had endured for the nine years of the abuse he saw me go through. Just thinking about how he cried telling me some years later, how he would sit in the window every time I leave with Jeff crying, wondering if I would come home alive. Now years had gone by, my son opened up to tell me how painful he felt. No child should have to go through so much pain. Son, I am so sorry. You carried this burden for all these years! I was so wrapped up at that time, trying to survive and keep my pain from him that he never talked about it until years later. We cried together as he lived through his pain. Son, please forgive me!

Now praying and seeking God about how to tell Mickis (which was due to come home from college) about

Billy. Asking God also, Is this my Boaz? My covering and my best friend?

About three weeks of Billy going to church with me, one Sunday at the end of service, pastor had the altar call. Billy got up and went forward for salvation. (Thank you, Jesus.) He got baptized in Jesus's name. He tarried for the Holy Ghost that Sunday, but he didn't receive God's spirit that day. He kept reading scriptures and asking question about the Bible, so every Wednesday and Sunday, he would come forward for someone to lay their hands on him and tarry with him for the Holy Ghost. At this time, we were becoming really good friends! He kept saying, "One of these days, I am going to marry you." I would just smile. In my heart, I knew what I had prayed for and waited to hear from God. He was truly a gentleman, never tried to have sex with me. (Thank you, Jesus.)

December 31, 1995, it was a Sunday night right before midnight, Billy received the Holy Ghost with the evidence of speaking in tongues. It was the first time I saw Billy cry. After he received God's spirit, He spoke in tongues the new year's in! The next few days, Billy asked me to date him, and of course, I said yes! A few days after, he came into the commissary, and I looked up to see him coming toward me. My heart skipped a beat and fluttered. It scared me. My mind went back to what I prayed some weeks ago! Mickis was home now, and I invited Billy over for dinner so he could meet my son. After dinner, I exited the room so they could talk. Billy assured Mickis, "I would never hit your mother. I will protect her and provide for her."

A few days later, Billy asked for my father's phone number. The next day, he called my dad and asked if he would give him permission to marry his daughter (me). My mouth flew open. My father said yes for 50 cents! Then Billy asked my son, Mickis, if he could marry me. Some days later, I invited Billy over to have dinner with me. After we finished dinner, he got down on one knee and asked me to marry him. Still, one piece of my pray request was not giving to me yet, which was the word backing it up!

Something I've always remembered Pastor Swancy saying, "Before you make a decision, (1) *Are the circumstances right?* (2) *Do you have peace with it?* (3) *Does the word back it up?* I don't remember what scriptures they were now, but that Sunday at church, Pastor quoted them. Driving home from church that night, I said "Yes, I will marry you." I met Billy in October 1995; we got married on March 8, 1996, at Peace Apostolic Church on a Friday night. My son, Mickis, walked me down the aisle and presented me to Billy without a spot on my dress because we never had sex before marriage.

(Thank you, Jesus.) We had a Marine Corp wedding, which included tapping my behind with the sword!

ROSE HOGANS

Notes

A SAINT, A WIFE,
A MOTHER, AND
A FRIEND

It had been a great journey of stretching, growing, learning, and discovering how to heal, who I am, and who I hope to be as a child of God, wife, and real mother to my children Mickis, Malinda, and Bryan. (Billy had two children when we got married.). I am still a work in progress, willing to grow more in the things of God. Lots of hard knocks through the years, but the good outweighs the bad, with Jesus on my side and being my everything. A saying I ask daily, *"Jesus take full control."* "I love you, Lord Jesus, you are my everything. The Lord is mighty in power, my fortress and my deliver; my God is my rock, in whom I take refuge, my shield and the horn of my salvation, my stronghold" (Psalm 18:1–2 NIV).

There is so much more to tell about Rose's life. It's by God's mercy and grace that I am still alive to tell my story. Through the many scars, there are much more stars! Letting go of your hurts and pains will help you *grow* so you can *glow* so you can *go*! <u>Be honest</u>! Admit you need help. Take off the mask. Trust God for the results. Identify who or what is causing you hurt/pain. <u>Talk about it</u>! Look at that person in the mirror (which is you). Take the necessary steps to heal. Forgive those you feel have hurt you or caused you pain, and remember that you are never alone! God is always there; he never *"sleeps or slumbers… I lift up my eyes to the hills—where does my help come from? My help comes from the Lord, the Maker of heaven and earth. He will not let your foot slip—he who watches over you will not slumber* (Psalm 121:1–3 NIV). Life is so precious. God gave it to each of us. Stand tall and stand firm. God has ways we know not of! Trusting him makes a world of difference. *"Cast all your anxiety [worries, fears] on him because he cares for you"* (1 Peter 5:7 NIV).

It's because of him I am able to smile, to have peace that passes all understanding, to deal with self-esteem issues, to encourage others sincerely from the heart, and to have confidence that I once didn't have. God is amazing and always has our best interest at heart. There's no greater love than Jesus! He is consistent, patient, and He is so kind. His love never fails! He loved us to death! Death on the cross! "Better is one day in your courts than a thousand elsewhere; I would rather be a doorkeeper in the house of my God than dwell in the tents of the wicked" (Psalms 84:10 NIV). So much more to share!

Notes

TURNS IN MY LIFE

How my mother was murdered less than a year later after returning to Arkansas, on January 27, 1997. After all these years, we still don't know who murdered our mother!

How marrying Billy on March 8, 1996, changed my life.

How Billy and I lost everything about eight years into our marriage.

How my honey got robbed at gunpoint and how intercessory prayer worked in that situation.

How the Lord opened so many doors for us and He overwhelmed us on many occasions.

How my husband, Billy, battled through cancer three times.

How I was my husband's caregiver, nurse, wife, and best friend.

How my husband worked right up to the last day of his life here on earth.

So much more to tell about God's blessing, kindness, and patience with us.

How Billy and I weathered through many tests and trials.

How the Lord gave Billy and me twenty-four years, one month, two weeks, and ten days of marriage before my honey went to be with the Lord on April 30, 2020, after battling cancer thrice.

Life is so precious. Take the time to tell someone you love them. Give words of affirmation, give gifts of yourself, spend quality time with each other, and give physical touch. Do random acts of kindness. I was just thinking over my twenty-four-plus years with Billy. We had many ups and downs, but the good outweighed the bad. No matter what, we stuck together—through thick and thin, for better or for worse, for richer or for poorer, in sickness and in health, till death did us part. We experienced each stage of our wedding vows, looking forward to telling the next journey of my life.

Remember this: with the Lord on your side, you can make it through anything if you put it into His hands— His mighty hands.

Here I am, telling my story of many beatings, so many near-death experiences and many blessing of all kinds and types, feeling fabulous, marvelous, and talented because of the love of Jesus! What a mighty, amazing friend, companion, also father I have in Jesus. Life is so sweet wrapped in Jesus! My life is a journey of many twists and turns, ups and downs, but I am still here, in Jesus's name. I have seen God do the impossible and still doing it until this day. It's an honor to give God glory and praises for His many, many benefits. If you *think* of Jesus, you would *thank* Jesus. We have so much to be thankful for! Grab a hold; there's much more to come.

I am a woman of God—"*For we are God's workmanship, created in Christ Jesus to do good works, which God prepared in advance for us to do*" (Ephesians 2:10 NIV). I don't have an amazing figure or a flattering body. I am far from being considered a model in the eyes of the world. I don't wear makeup or flashy things, but I am me, *learning to be set free!* I had scars, which Jesus has turned to stars. I am still a work in progress, saying to myself, "Caged no more," learning to be me!

I have a history, which I hope will be a great testimony to *help* many to see that God can do what we can't do, that God can take someone like me—with no high school diploma; who was abused, broken, and scarred; who thought she would amount to nothing. "*Then I [Jesus] passed by and saw you squirming in your own blood. You were covered with blood but I wouldn't let you die. I made you grow like a healthy plant. You grew strong and tall and became a young woman. Your breasts were well-formed, and your hair had grown, but you were naked*" (Ezekiel 16:6–7 GNT).

Some love me; maybe some hate me. I have done good and sometimes bad, but because of the love of Jesus, I still stand. I don't pretend to be someone I'm not. "I praise you because I am fearfully and wonderfully made; your works are wonderful, I know that full well" (Psalm 139:14 NIV).

I am who I am, learning to be who God has created me to be—a woman with purpose! I love each of you, and I love from the heart. I hope and pray that this book would be a blessing and healer to each who reads it! Your circumstances may appear hopeless, but nothing is impossible for

God! Your storms may seem big, *but God is bigger than the storm*!

My name is Rose, and this is part of my true story. Please pray for me.

I desire that God gets the glory in my life and throughout this book.

But the Lord says, Rose, "do not cling to events of the past or dwell on what happened long ago." (Isaiah 43:18 GNT).

Love can be blind in own our strength. *Prayer is key.*

God wants the *best* for each of us. God only gives the *best*. Can we wait patiently until he gives it? This is what the Lord says, "*Your redeemer, the Holy One of Israel: 'I am the Lord your God, who teaches you what is best for you, who directs you in the way you should go*" (Isaiah 48:17 NIV).

> *Remember you can make it through* Jesus by speaking life over your life.
> *Remember you can make it through* Jesus by speaking life over your life.
> *Remember you can make it through* Jesus by speaking life over your life.
> *So then faith cometh by hearing, and hearing by the word of God* (Romans 10:17 KJV).

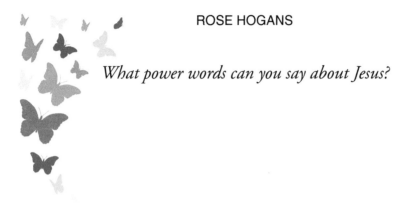

What power words can you say about Jesus?

ENDORSEMENTS

Thank you, Jesus, for allowing me to be here and to speak about my life. The Lord has always protected me. It was not easy sitting at a window wondering if my mother would return! When she did return, she was beaten and bruised and bloody. Should a little boy see that? All I know besides Jesus is how to survive. So what did we do? We survived, and we're here now because of the Lord. (Thank you, Jesus.) Please enjoy the book my mother has written. She has been through a lot. Be blessed beyond measure today in Jesus's name!

Love, MSB.

—Mickis Brown

Clips that I remember from my childhood. I remember being at a tender young age of between twelve to fourteen riding home (to Johnsville) with my dad, who was so drunk that he told me to drive. "Me driving us home?" I got behind the wheel and drove home just fine down the dirt road. I and another car coming toward me approached the wooden man-made bridge that was only wide enough for one vehicle. As I pulled over to the far right, I didn't realize that I pulled over too far toward the ditch to avoid a collision. The Lord allowed my wheel to hit a large rock that was embedded in the sand to keep the car from falling off the bridge. We all sat up real, still frozen in fear for a few minutes. We all eased out the opposite side of the car slowly. My father sobered up really quick and drove home the rest of the way. The Lord has been watching over me even before I learned about him.

Another clip. I think that I was about fourteen years old driving my father's old yellow-and-white Ford car (jalopy). I pulled up to park the car next to the butane tank outside of our house. I'm pumping the brakes and realized that I was pumping the paddle of the floor. The car is not stopping. Fear started to hit me! I was thinking to myself, _If I hit that thing full of butane (gas), it's going to blow up!_ Well, I did roll right into it because the car had no brakes. I was so scared that I parked that car and jumped out immediately and ran like crazy to safety. Another scary moment that the Lord protected me from.

Another clip. I remember my mom, Rose, and myself going to the store. My mom had very little money, so she bought us a Suzy Q to share and herself a pack of cigarettes. As we were walking home, somehow we ended up in the middle of a riot. We started running home. My shoes were so worn out that the seam had busted up the back. My shoes were already flapping when I walked. When I started running, I lost my shoe and started crying because I wanted to go back and get my shoe. My mom said, "Girl, come on." She grabbed my hand, and we ran home. I ran home wearing one shoe. Again, God's mercy and grace.

I do remember being in Hermitage High School at the age of sixteen when a recruiter from the USMC came to visit our school. I listened attentively because I wanted to get away from Johnsville, and I knew that my parents couldn't afford to send me to college. I thought to myself, *The military is my free ticket out.* So when I turned seventeen, I started the process of working with a recruiter to get down my weight limit, to pass the PT test and the ASVAB test. I hated to leave my sisters, but I figured if I go and make a better life for myself, I could help them to get away from Johnsville as well. So I joined the marine corps on June 24, 1980. I left for boot camp in Parris Island, South Carolina. I had to get away

because I saw the abuse my mom and sisters was going through. I wanted more, and I was determined to be able to help my family as much as possible.

May God bless you all.

—Lynda Brown

As I tell how I felt about seeing the abuse that my sister Rose and my mom suffered throughout the years, I asked God how to put it into words! I would first like to say I know that it is the grace and mercy of God that got me through it for years. I have seen my mom being beat by my dad for years, only to get out of the house to see my sister go through the same thing. If that wasn't enough, I was being molested at the same time for years. I was so scared to tell anyone about it, so I held the secret in over forty years. This still affects me to this day. I'm sharing this in hopes that this will help someone else to know they are not alone. Please free yourself of the hurt and pain. *It's not your fault.* Being abused or molested is something that can scar you and change the person that God meant for you to be. Please don't be a victim; be a victor! You can overcome this. Find someone to talk to, so you can be caged no more, learning to be set FREE.

God can free us from the things that enslave us, giving us the strength and courage to be set free.

—Gwen Morris-Drye

So if the Son sets you free, you will be free indeed. (John 8:36 NIV)

FAMILY PHOTOS

ABOUT THE AUTHOR

Rose Hogans is a humble woman of God with great faith, who is a prayer warrior and an altar worker; has a great burden for souls and really loves everyone; a business owner and an entrepreneur; is very purpose-driven, open-minded to new things; a mother; a widower; a sister; and a grandmother and friend to all. She lives in San Antonio, Texas, and was a nurse, wife, and caregiver for her late husband, Billy Hogans, who battle through cancer for the last eight years of his life.

Hope this book has inspired you, to know you can make it through Jesus!

The greatest gift you can give is your true story!
Trusting Jesus for the results.

CPSIA information can be obtained
at www.ICGtesting.com
Printed in the USA
BVHW011025030723
666714BV00018B/648